Felt-o-ween

Felt-o-ween

40 Scary-Cute Projects to Celebrate Halloween

KATHY SHELDON & AMANDA CARESTIO

LARK

An Imprint of Sterling Publishing
387 Park Avenue South
New York, NY 10016

ISBN 978-1-4547-0851-3

Library of Congress Cataloging-in-Publication Data

Sheldon, Kathy, 1959-
  Felt-o-ween : 40 scary-cute projects to celebrate Halloween / Kathy Sheldon.
     pages cm
  Includes bibliographical references and index.
  ISBN 978-1-4547-0851-3 (alk. paper)
  1. Halloween decorations. 2. Felt craft. I. Title.
TT900.H32S53 2014
745.594'1646--dc23
                              2013039868

Distributed in Canada by Sterling Publishing
c/o Canadian Manda Group, 165 Dufferin Street
Toronto, Ontario, Canada M6K 3H6
Distributed in the United Kingdom by GMC Distribution Services
Castle Place, 166 High Street, Lewes, East Sussex, England BN7 1XU
Distributed in Australia by Capricorn Link (Australia) Pty. Ltd.
P.O. Box 704, Windsor, NSW 2756, Australia

For information about custom editions, special sales, and premium and corporate purchases, please
contact Sterling Special Sales at 800-805-5489 or specialsales@sterlingpublishing.com.

Email academic@larkbooks.com for information about desk and examination copies.
The complete policy can be found at larkcrafts.com.

Manufactured in China

2 4 6 8 10 9 7 5 3 1

larkcrafts.com

Contents

Don't worry: We're not going to make you wade through yet another summary of the historical roots of Halloween. As far as we're concerned, Halloween equals one thing: FUN. And when we think fun, we think felt!

Are you too old to trick-or-treat but you want to get in on the fun? Or maybe you're looking for a costume for your little one? Felt is your friend. Excited about an upcoming costume party, but stumped about what to wear? Reach for the felt. Dying to dress your nest with unique, yet marvelously spooky (and handmade!) décor items? Frighteningly fun and festive, felt is the fabric that's got you (and your house) covered when it comes to Halloween.

Perhaps you're a fan of our (how can we put this modestly?) incredibly popular book *Fa la la la Felt*, so you already know what our stellar group of designers can do when combining felt and Christmas. Or maybe you own *Heart-Felt Holidays*, and you've been crafting up felt goodness throughout the year. You won't be disappointed when you see what this same group has come up with given the chance to fill 132 pages with felt Halloween projects.

We've got wee witch booties for the barely toddling, animal ear headbands for cute critter getups, or an undead choker if you're going the gruesome route. If it's your home you plan on dressing up instead, you'll find garlands, bat pillows, a bug-strewn wreath, and a pumpkin-headed old-timey band for your mantle. If you're throwing a party, check out the monster ring toss, pumpkin party treat pouches, graveyard-themed cupcake toppers, festive napkins, and even a black cat candleholder with glowing eyes.

Let your kids pick out a project for you to make for them or (better yet) have them help. We've got a plush vampire for them to snuggle with, two different treat bags to hold their candy stash, monster hands to make them feel enormous, and a pirate eye patch that lifts up to reveal a ghoulish scar.

A few of the projects are no-sew, and many can be stitched up by hand. If you're new to felt or need a refresher on some techniques, check out the Basics section, starting on page 7. If you want to jump right in and craft, you'll find the projects with supplies listed and step-by-step instructions starting on page 16—and all templates called for are in the back of the book, starting on page 110. Grab your felt, turn the pages, and get your spooktacular felt craftiness on!

Felt Basics

There is nothing scary about crafting with felt—any zombie with half a brain can do it! Felt is both the beginning sewer's dream material and (as you can see in this book) an endless source of inspiration for experienced designers. In this section we'll cover the materials, tools, and techniques used to create the Halloween projects that follow. Chances are good that you already have most of the materials and tools you'll need on hand. A quick trip to a fabric or craft store or a little online shopping should take care of the rest. Check the list in the Basic Sewing Kit (page 9) and then skim the What You Need list before beginning a project. A number of the projects call for embroidery stitches: You'll find a guide to all of them starting on page 12.

Basic Materials

FELT

Felt is easy to cut, sew, and embellish, and is beloved by crafters because it doesn't fray. This means that all sorts of rather boring things that you have to do with most fabrics to take care of the fraying factor are unnecessary with felt, and that means more time for the fun stuff!

Head to the felt section of a fabric or craft store (or look online), and you'll see that the range of colors and types of felt available is enough to make your head spin. You can find hand-dyed wool felt, wool/rayon felt, acrylic felt, eco felt made from post-consumer recycled plastic bottles, and even felt made from bamboo and rayon. It comes as sheets (usually known as craft felt) or as yardage and in both solid colors and patterns. You can even buy handy adhesive-backed felt sheets like the ones used for the Bat Mobile on page 46.

Wool Felt

One hundred percent wool is the thickest and sturdiest felt. It usually comes in beautiful, subtle (and often hand-dyed) colors. It won't tear apart or pill the way acrylic felt sometimes does. Wool felt is more expensive than acrylic or wool blend felt, and it's harder to find in-store (you can, however, find plenty of wool felt online). Because of the cost, we tend to save our 100 percent wool felt for smaller, special projects.

Wool Blend Felt

Wool blend felt is similar to 100 percent wool felt and comes in many of the same warm, subtle colors. The addition of synthetic fibers makes the felt more flexible, so it's easier to sew and drapes a little better than pure wool felt. Wool blend felt costs less than wool felt but more than acrylic felt. If you can't find wool blend felt at your local craft or fabric store, you can purchase it online.

Acrylic Felt

Acrylic felt (sold in both sheets and as yardage) is made by pressing tiny acrylic fibers together until they interlock into a mat of material. It's inexpensive, widely available, and fade resistant. It's washable, too, so use it for projects like the Day of the Dead Kid's Tee on page 78. But acrylic felt is usually thinner—and therefore more transparent—than wool or wool blend felt. This kind of felt is fine for most projects, but it can stretch out of shape, open up at seams and stitch holes (especially in stuffed projects or projects subject to a lot of stress), and get fuzzy if handled a lot. We've found that as felt has become more popular and widely available, the quality of acrylic felt has also started to vary greatly, so hold each sheet or bolt of felt up to the light and examine it before buying—felt that's so thin that it's transparent won't work well for some projects.

Eco Felt

Made from post-consumer plastic bottles, eco felt shares almost all of acrylic felt's characteristics, but it is reusing something that might otherwise clog the landfills. Another added benefit of acrylic and eco felt is that people who are allergic to wool or are averse to using products that come from animals prefer to craft with them.

Bamboo Felt

Bamboo felt is typically 50 percent bamboo and 50 percent rayon. This makes it a very soft, natural material that is also vegan. If you can't find bamboo felt at your local craft store, look online.

Adhesive-Backed Felt

Adhesive-backed felt sheets come in handy for some no-sew projects (such as the Bat Mobile on page 46). The sticky stuff on the back of these felt sheets can gunk up scissors or needles used to cut or pierce the felt. A quick swipe from a cotton ball dipped in nail polish remover should take care of the problem.

Wool Roving

The Felted Fall Acorns (page 96) call for wool roving. This is carded wool drawn into long continuous strands. You can find it online and in many craft stores. The project instructions explain how to felt with this material.

THREAD AND FLOSS

We've learned that when it comes to thread, it's worth it to spend a little bit more and purchase a quality polyester, cotton/polyester blend, or all-cotton thread for machine and hand stitching. It makes sewing much easier and creates strong seams that stay strong.

For decorative embroidery stitches, your best bet is embroidery floss, available in just about every shade of every color you can imagine at craft and fabric stores. A strand of embroidery floss is usually made up of six individual threads twisted together. Many projects call for using just two or three of the strands. To separate strands without a tangled mess, hold the ends of the number of strands desired, and then very *slowly* pull these away from the rest of the threads in the strand.

STUFFING

If our project instructions tell you to stuff it, you can use polyester fiberfill, cotton batting, wool roving, or even sewing scraps. The Sew Gross Hand Warmers on page 73 are stuffed with rice so they can be heated in a microwave.

EMBELLISHMENTS AND DOODADS

Before you head out to shop, look through the projects you want to make, and note any buttons, ribbon, sequins, rickrack, etc., that you'll need. Of course, part of the fun of creating is doing your own thing, so feel free to think of the embellishments we've used as suggestions and substitute freely.

ADHESIVES

Fabric glue, craft glue, tacky glue, spray adhesive, and temporary spray adhesive are called for in some of these projects. If you don't have what's listed, just test whatever adhesive you do have on some felt scraps before substituting.

Basic Tools

You don't need a lot of tools to make the projects in this book. Many can be sewn by hand and a few don't require any sewing at all. Take a look at the Basic Sewing Kit (on left), and then look at the What You Need list for each project before you start.

Basic Sewing Kit

scissors

pinking or scallop shears

template transfer paper (tissue, copier, or freezer paper)

straight pins

hand-sewing needles

embroidery needles & hoop

iron

ruler

craft & fabric glue

fabric pen

sewing machine (optional)

rotary cutting tools (optional)

Basic Techniques

Most of the same techniques you use with other sewing projects will work when sewing felt; in fact, felt is usually easier to work with than other fabrics!

TRANSFERRING TEMPLATES

All of the templates for the projects can be found starting on page 110. Transferring templates to felt (especially dark Halloweeny colors) can be tricky. Here are some of the techniques we use:

Freezer Paper Method

Our favorite way to transfer templates to felt is by using freezer paper and an iron. Freezer paper (available in most supermarkets near the foil and plastic wrap) has a waxy side that, when ironed, allows it to temporarily stick to felt and then be removed without leaving any residue. Here are the steps:

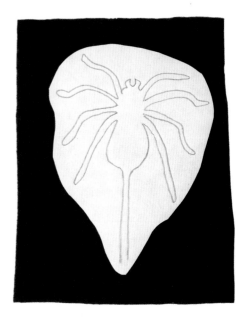

1. Trace the template at the correct size onto the plain (unwaxed) side of the freezer paper (this paper is transparent enough that you should be able to see through it; if not, hold the template and freezer paper against a window to trace). Make sure you are drawing on the correct side of the paper—if you iron the waxy side, you'll have a sticky mess on your iron!

2. Cut around the outside of the traced template, making sure to leave a border of freezer paper.

3. Place the template onto your felt, waxy side down, and with use an iron at a low setting with no steam to adhere the template to the felt.

4. Cut along the traced lines to cut out the shape, and then remove the freezer paper.

Tissue Paper Method

For patterns with embroidery designs, enlarge the template to the appropriate size, and then trace the template (including any embroidery patterns) onto a piece of tissue paper. Pin the tissue paper in place on the felt piece to be embroidered. Embroider the designs (through both the felt and the paper). When finished, cut out the felt shape and tear away the tissue paper. You may need to use a sewing needle or tweezers to pull out any tiny pieces stuck under your stitches.

Enlarge & Transfer Method

If you don't have freezer paper, for medium to large pattern pieces in simple shapes, just enlarge the template to the appropriate size and cut it out. Then pin this template onto the felt, and cut around it to cut out the shape. For especially small or intricate shapes, cut out the paper template, pin it to the felt, and then use a disappearing fabric marker to trace around the template, directly onto the felt. (Test your fabric markers on a piece of scrap felt first—some "disappear" better than others.) Use the traced lines to cut. Disappearing fabric markers can also be used with light-colored felt to trace embroidery lines. Just place the felt on top of the pattern and trace the stitch lines with the marker. (For intricate embroidery patterns that may take a while to complete, use a water-soluble fabric marker instead of a disappearing one.)

FINISHING FELT

Have we made it clear enough that we love the fact that felt doesn't fray? This means the edges of your projects can be finished (or not) in all kinds of different ways:

- It takes nothing more than the swipe of the right shears to get felt scalloped or pinked edges in projects like Mollie Johanson's Spooky Friends Wall Hanging (page 34).

- The blanket stitch creates a look that says "made by hand and proud of it." See the Day of the Dead Kid's Tee (page 78).

- Machine stitch around the outside edge of your felt pieces for the polished look you'll see in Dana Willard's Batty Pillows (page 106).

- For machine-stitched edge with pizzazz, try the zigzag stitch Cynthia Shaffer used for her Wee Witch Booties (page 32).

- For an "unfinished finish," use a straight (or running) stitch near the edge of the felt and leave the edges raw like Jody Rackley did with her Zombie Candy Corn Plushie (page 87).

- Or skip the stitching altogether and just go with cut edges: See the Undead Chokers & Bracelets (page 80).

EMBROIDERY STITCHES

Embroidery and felt go together like devils and pitchforks. Use these illustrations to help you with any unfamiliar stitches or feel free to substitute your own favorite stitch.

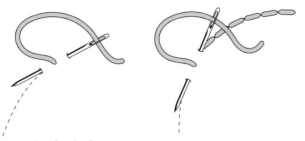

Backstitch

This simple stitch creates a solid line, so it's great for outlining shapes or creating text.

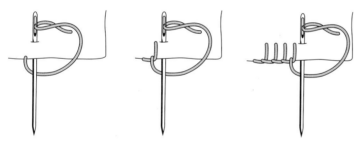

Blanket Stitch

The blanket stitch is both decorative and functional. Use this stitch to accentuate an edge or to attach an appliqué.

Blind Stitch

If you don't want your stitches to show, blind stitch is the best way to join two pieces of fabric or to close up openings.

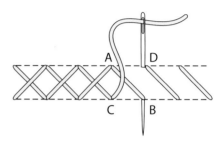

Cross Stitch

Start by making a straight stitch from A to B. Make a second straight stitch from C to D. If you're making a row of cross stitches, you can first make a row of the underlying stitches (A to B) and then go back and cross them all at once.

French Knot

This elegant little knot adds interest and texture when embroidering or embellishing.

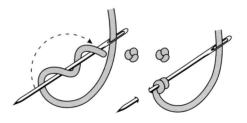

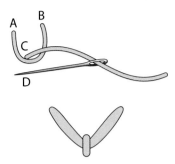

Open Loop (or Fly) Stitch
To make this decorative stitch, first make a loose horizontal stitch from A to B. Press the loop flat to one side with a finger. Bring the needle back up at C, in the center of the stitch. Return the needle at D.

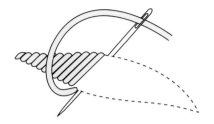

Satin Stitch
The satin stitch is composed of parallel rows of straight stitches and is often used to fill in an outline.

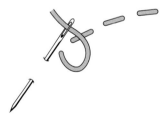

Straight (or Running) Stitch
Make this stitch by weaving the needle through the fabric at evenly spaced intervals.

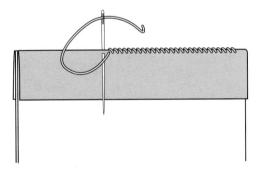

Whipstitch
Also called the overcast stitch, the whipstitch is used to bind edges to prevent raveling or for decorative purposes. Simply stitch over the edge of the fabric.

Spooky or kooky? Gruesome or sweet? Make your Halloween special with these felt treats. A friendly ghost here, a flying bat there, and lots of candy corn everywhere.

Creepy Crawly Wreath

DESIGNER: LAURA HOWARD

Welcome October—and your guests!—with this yarn-wrapped wreath featuring felt bugs peeking out from behind autumn leaves and a silly spooky spider dangling from its web.

WHAT YOU NEED

Basic sewing kit (page 9)

Templates (page 112)

Large half-ring foam wreath, 14 inches (35.6 cm)

1 or 2 skeins of bulky yarn in black

1 skein of light worsted yarn in white

Felt scraps in dark gray, light gray, brown, pale brown, and a selection of autumnal shades (for the leaves)

Embroidery floss in white and various colors to match the leaves

2 black felt sheets, 9 x 12 inches (22.9 x 30.5 cm)

White and black sewing thread

Black seed beads (sizes 8/0 and 9/0)

Tape (optional)

Glue gun and glue

WHAT YOU DO

1 Secure the end of a ball of black yarn to the wreath form by tying a knot or using a piece of sticky tape. Wrap the yarn around the wreath form a dozen or so times, then bunch up the yarn so it thickly covers a narrow segment of the wreath. Repeat this process over and over, so that the wreath is gradually covered with an even amount of yarn. When the whole wreath is covered, knot the loose end of yarn securely at the back of the wreath and weave in the end neatly.

2 Use the templates provided to cut out an assortment of leaves in autumnal shades. The number of leaves required will vary depending on the size of your wreath. Using the bug templates A through F, cut out as many bugs and small spiders as you want to add to the wreath. Arrange the pieces on the wreath as you cut them out, using pins to hold each piece in place as you build up the design.

3 Add veins to the leaves using embroidery floss in coordinating colors. For each leaf, cut a length of floss, split the strands in half, and use the lines marked on the templates as a rough guide for your stitching. Sew a line down the center of each leaf with backstitch, and use straight stitch to add the side veins to the larger leaves, sewing out from the central line and then back again to create a continuous line of stitching.

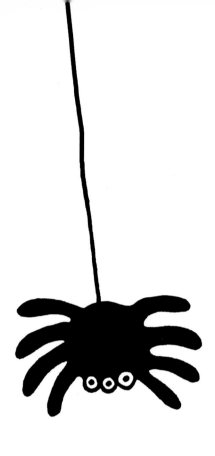

4 Sew each bug shape onto a backing piece of black felt, using matching sewing thread and whipstitches. Then for each bug, use split floss (in a matching color) to add legs and feelers to the bugs, using the legs shown on the template pages as a guide.

5 Add black seed beads to each bug for eyes, sewing each bead flat like an "O" with three or four stitches of black sewing thread. Use size 9/0 beads for bugs A, B and C, and larger size 8/0 beads for the others.

6 Cut out all the bugs. Trim the black backing felt around each bug to a neat, rounded shape, and take care not to cut too close to your stitching.

7 Cut out the spiderweb shape from black felt, using the template provided. Then use a large sharp needle and lengths of white yarn to create the spiderweb design on the black felt, using the web drawn on the template as a rough guide. Sew one long stitch for each spoke, then sew the yarn in place by sewing small stitches along it with white sewing thread. Then add the lines around the web: sew a single stitch between each spoke, gently pulling the yarn into a curved shape and using more stitches to hold it in position. Do not carry any thread or yarn along the back of the shape. Finish the web by adding a length of yarn at the point marked on the template (the spider will dangle from this later).

Note: If you prefer, use white floss and the tracing paper transfer method to stitch the web shape on black felt instead.

8 Cut away the excess felt around the web and some of the felt from within the web itself, as indicated by the dotted lines on the templates. To cut the felt away from the inside, fold the felt in half, cut a small hole, and then cut outward from this hole, taking care not to cut into any of your stitching.

9 Use the templates provided to cut out the pieces for the spider: two black spider bodies, two black spider legs, and four white spider eyes. Pin the leg pieces together, and use black sewing thread to sew the legs together with whipstitch and the body section together with straight stitch. Remove the pin.

10 Decorate one spider body piece, sewing the eyes on in a row with white sewing thread and whipstitch. Add a black seed bead (size 8/0) to each eye to form the pupils, sewing each bead flat like an "O" with three or four stitches of black sewing thread. Then use a piece of split white floss to stitch two V-shaped fangs for the spider's mouth. If you'd prefer to make a happy spider, use backstitch to sew a curved smile.

11 Arrange all the leaves and bugs on the wreath so the leaves slightly overlap the bugs. Take a digital photo or draw a sketch

of your finished arrangement, remove all the pieces, and lay them out next to the wreath. Then use a glue gun to adhere them to the wreath one by one to build up the design.

12 Glue the spiderweb in place, starting by gluing the center and working outward. The web should be positioned on the wreath so the dangling piece of yarn is hanging down from the top center of the wreath.

13 Attach the spider to the wreath, sewing through the center of the sewn-together leg pieces with the dangling piece of yarn. Before making your stitches, hold up the wreath to check that the spider hangs where you want it to. Trim any excess yarn. Then add the front and back spider pieces, and sew around the body with black whipstitches, sewing the layers together. Finish your stitching neatly at the back.

There's something so cheery about the colors of candy corn! Use these instructions and alternate felt colors for different celebrations throughout the year.

Candy Corn Bunting

WHAT YOU NEED

TO MAKE 8 FLAGS

Basic sewing kit (page 9)

Templates (page 118)

5 yellow felt sheets, 9 x 12 inches (22.9 x 30.5 cm)

Orange felt, 7 x 8½ inches (17.8 x 21.6 cm)

White felt, 5 x 6½ inches (12.7 x 16.5 cm)

Yellow, orange, and white sewing thread

Yellow bias binding, 1 inch (2.5 cm) wide and 8 feet (2.4 m) long

WHAT YOU DO

1 Use the templates provided to cut out the felt pieces for all the bunting flags. For each flag, cut two yellow flag shapes, one yellow top piece, one orange middle piece, and one white bottom piece.

Note: Depending on the length you'd like your bunting to be, you might need to make additional flags. This sample was created with eight flags.

2 Pin the white bottom piece onto one of the yellow flag shapes. Use white sewing thread to sew a line of straight stitch along the top edge of the white felt.

3 Pin the orange middle piece on the flag, and sew it in position with straight stitch and orange thread along the top and bottom edges.

4 Pin the yellow top piece in place, and secure it with a line of yellow straight stitch along the bottom edge. Remove all the pins.

5 Place the finished flag shape on another yellow flag, and pin the layers together. Use yellow sewing thread to sew a line of straight stitch down one side of the triangle and up the other side, sewing the three layers of felt together. Remove the pins.

6 Repeat steps 2 through 5 to make the rest of the flags.

7 Fold the binding over the top edge of each triangle and pin it in place, sandwiching the felt between the folded binding. Arrange the flags so they're next to each other, as pictured, or leave gaps between the flags to make a longer bunting. Make sure you leave plenty of extra binding at each end of your bunting so you can hang it up later.

8 At one end, open the binding and fold the cut end inward. Then fold the binding again (the cut end should now be hidden inside the folded binding) and pin it together, working down the binding until you reach the flags. Repeat this for the other end of the binding.

9 Sew the edges of the binding together with a line of yellow straight stitch, sewing through the tops of the felt flags as you sew past them. Work gradually along the bunting from one end to the other, removing the pins as you sew.

Bat Socks

DESIGNER: CYNTHIA SHAFFER

Sure, your kid will want a pair of these adorable appliquéd socks, but don't you want to make a pair for yourself while you're at it?

WHAT YOU NEED

Basic sewing kit (page 9)

Template (page 110)

13 x 6-inch (33 x 15.2 cm) piece of cardboard

Tall knee-high socks in gray and white stripes

Black felt scraps

Temporary spray adhesive

Black perle cotton floss

Hand-sewing needle

WHAT YOU DO

1 Use the cardboard to make a stretcher form for the sock. It will be much easier to stitch on when stretched taut.

Note: The top bat needs to be stitched while on the cardboard form because the sock is stretched out the most at this upper area and the bat will lie flat, which makes it easy to stitch onto the sock. For the remaining bats, the sock is not very stretched out and the bats are easier to stitch with the sock off the template.

2 Using the template, cut out six bats from the black felt.

3 Slip one sock up onto the cardboard form.

4 Use the spray adhesive to attach three bats to the back of the sock.

5 Stitch the top bat to the sock with black perle cotton floss and a hand-sewing needle. Use a whipstitch (page 13). Add a few extra stitches to the head of the bat to look like ears.

6 Slip the sock off of the template, and sew the remaining bats to the sock.

7 Repeat steps 3 through 6 for the second sock.

Need a wee witch hat? Or a sassy costume accent for yourself? This fascinator fits the bill.

Wicked Sassy Fascinator

DESIGNER: AMANDA CARESTIO

WHAT YOU NEED

Basic sewing kit (page 9)

Templates (page 127)

2 black felt sheets, 9 x 12 inches (22.9 x 30.5 cm)

Felt scraps in dark gray and magenta

Pinking shears

5½ to 6-inch (14 to 15.2 cm) plate (for tracing the brim)

Black, light gray, and magenta embroidery floss

Black elastic strapping, about 24 inches (61 cm)

Note: To give your hat shape, it helps to work with firmer felt. Or you can stuff the hat shape with fiberfill; see the Tip on the right.

WHAT YOU DO

1 Use the templates to cut out one cone shape from black felt and one buckle from dark gray felt. Also, cut one 9 x 1-inch (22.9 x 2.5 cm) strip from magenta felt with pinking shears and, using your plate, two circle shapes from black felt.

2 Fold the cone around so the long straight edges meet, overlapping the layers slightly. Whipstitch the edge to itself with three strands of black floss, leaving the tail of floss attached; you'll use this to attach the cone to the hat base. Trim off the excess to flatten the bottom of the cone so it will sit flush.

Tip: If your felt isn't firm, stuff the cone with fiberfill or felt scraps to give it shape before moving to the next step.

3 Position the cone in the center of one of the black circle shapes and whipstitch it in place. Don't worry too much about neat stitches; these will be covered by the buckle and the hatband.

4 Stitch along each long edge of the magenta strip with light gray floss and long straight stitches, leaving the tail of floss attached. Thread the band through the buckle, wrap it around the cone, and stitch the end to itself and to the cone.

5 Fold the other circle in half, and cut two small slits 1½ inches (3.8 cm) in from each edge. Thread the elastic through the slits.

6 Sandwich and pin the two circles together, making sure the buckle will be facing front. Blanket-stitch around the edge with magenta floss.

7 Tie the ends of elastic together.

Give your favorite candle a place to rest and surround it with the sweetest spooks you've ever seen.

Ghosties Candle Mat

DESIGNER: MOLLIE JOHANSON

WHAT YOU NEED

Basic sewing kit (page 9)

Template (page 122)

Purple felt, 9 inches (22.9 cm) square

Charcoal gray felt, 8 inches (20.3 cm) square

White felt, about 6 inches (15.2 cm) square

Black, purple, and white embroidery floss

Scallop or pinking shears

Orange jumbo rickrack

WHAT YOU DO

1 Use the template to cut out five ghost shapes from white felt. Stitch their faces using three strands of black floss. Use French knots for the eyes and backstitch for the mouths.

2 From purple felt, cut out a circle that is about 8 inches (20.3 cm) across (see Tip). From charcoal gray felt and using scallop or pinking shears, cut out a circle that is about 7½ inches (19 cm) across.

Tip: Tracing the inside and outside of an 8-inch (20.3 cm) embroidery hoop works well for the circles needed in step 2.

3 Place the smaller felt circle on top of the larger circle, then stitch them together around the edge using three strands of purple floss and straight stitch. Position the ghosts so they are flying around the circle, and then stitch them in place using three strands of purple floss and straight stitch.

4 Stitch twinkling stars around the ghosts using three strands of white floss.

5 Attach the rickrack around the underside of the purple circle's edge using three strands of black floss and straight stitch.

Punkin' Treat Pouch

DESIGNER: MOLLIE JOHANSON

Fill these gleeful little gourds with treats to give out to trick-or-treaters or the guests at your Halloween party.

WHAT YOU NEED

Basic sewing kit page (page 9)

Templates (page 117)

Orange felt, about 5 x 7 inches (12.7 x 17.8 cm)

Felt scraps in black and green

Black and yellow embroidery floss

WHAT YOU DO

1 Using the templates, cut out one pumpkin front and two pumpkin backs from orange felt. Cut the pumpkin face pieces from black felt, and cut the stem from green felt.

2 Stitch the face pieces onto the front piece using three strands of black floss and straight stitch.

3 With the pumpkin facedown, place the two back pieces on the back so that the outside edges line up and the center edges overlap. Position the stem at the top, between the front and back layers. Pin the layers in place.

4 Stitch around the pumpkin shape using six strands of yellow embroidery floss and straight stitch. Be sure to catch the stem in your stitching.

5 Fill the pouch with treats (or maybe even a little trick!).

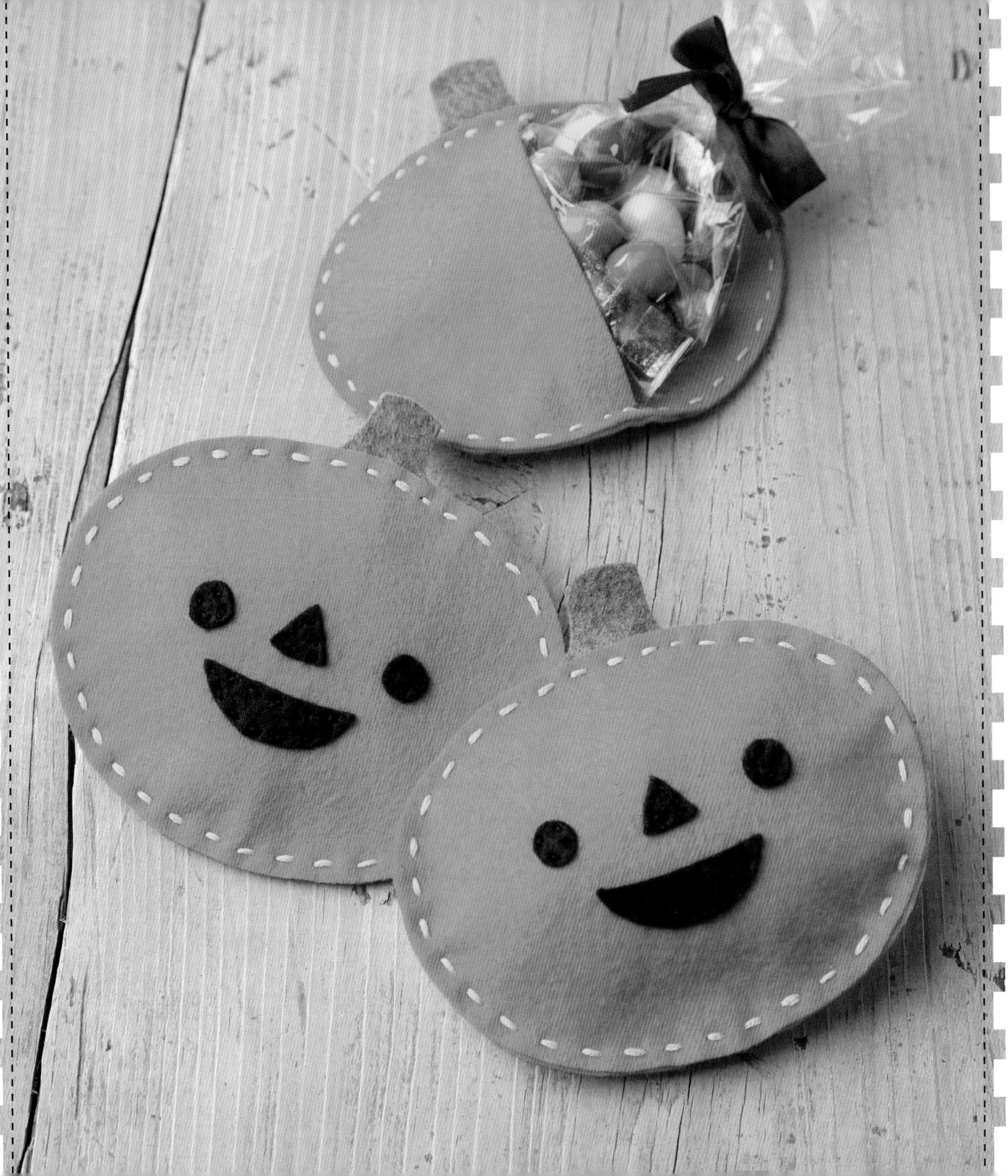

Whether these birds call to mind Alfred Hitchcock or Edgar Allen Poe, you'll want a flock of them with their beady little eyes to greet your guests this Halloween.

The Birds

DESIGNER: CYNTHIA SHAFFER

TO MAKE ONE

Basic sewing kit (page 9)

Templates (page 119)

2 black felt sheets, 9 x 12 inches (22.9 x 30.5 cm)

Yellow floss

Large-eye hand-sewing needle

Black floss

Fiberfill

2 black pipe cleaners, 12 inches (30.5 cm) long

Sandpaper, 100 grit

Wood block, 3½ x 3½ x 3½ inches (8.9 x 8.9 x 8.9 cm)

Drill and ½-inch (1.3 cm) drill bit

White paint

Paintbrush

Purple paint

Stick with 45° angle, 3¾ inches (9.5 cm) long with an arm that measures 3½ inches (8.9 cm) and 1¾ inches (4.4 cm) in circumference

Wood glue (optional)

Wire cutters

WHAT YOU DO

1 Trace the bird template onto paper and cut out.

2 Stack the two pieces of black felt on top of each other.

3 Pin the bird template onto the black felt and cut out. Transfer the eye placement mark. Stitch a French knot (page 12) at the eye placement mark on both sides using the yellow floss and the large-eye hand-sewing needle.

4 Stitch around the birds, through both layers, with a straight stitch using the black floss. Start near the legs, stitch across the body, around the head, and then down the opposite side. Leave an opening at the legs.

Note: Leave the needle and thread attached to the bird.

5 Lightly stuff the blackbird with a small amount of fiberfill.

6 Cut the black pipe cleaners in half so you now have four pieces that measure 6 inches (15.2 cm) each.

7 Grip two pipe cleaners at one end and twist, leaving 1 inch (2.5 cm) still splayed out. Continue twisting for 2 inches (5 cm).

8 Repeat step 7 to make the second leg.

9 Insert 1 inch (2.5 cm) of the short splayed-out leg into the bird. Repeat for the second leg.

10 Continue stitching along the leg openings of the bird, taking smaller stitches to secure the pipe cleaner legs.

11 Lightly sand the block.

12 Drill a hole into the center of the block.

13 Apply a thin layer of white paint. Let dry.

14 Apply a thin layer of purple paint to the block. Let dry.

15 Lightly sand the wood block until some of the white paint starts to show through.

16 Insert the stick into the hole. Glue in place with wood glue if needed.

17 Wrap the bird feet around the stick, adding a slight bend at the knees. Trim the feet with wire cutters if they seem too long.

Whether she's being a good witch or a bad witch that day, your little one will cackle with delight over these adorable felt lace-up booties!

Wee Witch Booties

DESIGNER: CYNTHIA SHAFFER

WHAT YOU NEED

Basic sewing kit (page 9)

Templates (page 120)

**2 black felt sheets, 9 x 12 inches
(22.9 x 30.5 cm)**

**Purple felt sheet, 9 x 12 inches
(22.9 x 30.5 cm)**

**Purple rattail cord (24 inches [61 cm] cut
into two 12-inch [30.5 cm] lengths)**

12 gold eyelet grommets, 5/32 inch (4 mm)

Fiberfill

WHAT YOU DO

1 Cut out two pairs of template A from black felt. Clip the notches and transfer all the markings.

2 Cut out the two template B shapes from black felt. Clip notches.

3 Cut out four template C shapes from black felt.

4 Cut out two template D shapes from purple felt. Mark the center back.

5 Place the template C shape on the wrong side of the template A shape at the center front.

6 Using a zigzag stitch, machine-stitch across the top and then down the front edge where the shapes overlap. Repeat for the other template A shape.

7 With right sides together stitch the template A shapes together at the center back seam, using a ¼-inch (6 mm) seam allowance.

8 Open up this seam and then stitch each side of the seam allowance down, close to the stitched seam.

9 Zigzag stitch around the front edge and the outer curve of the purple bootie cuff.

10 Align the cuff to the top edge of the bootie, and zigzag stitch it in place. Back tack at the beginning and at the end.

11 With right sides together, pin the bootie together at the top foot seam starting at the notch at the front opening, continuing to the toe point, and then to the notch under the toe curve. Stitch, using a ¼-inch (6 mm) seam allowance, back tacking at the beginning and at the end. Trim away the seam allowance at the point.

12 Pin the sole to the bootie, matching the center front and center back notches. Stitch in place.

13 Turn the bootie to the right side and poke out the pointy toe.

14 Set the eyelet grommets at the center front markings.

15 Stuff the toe with a small amount of fiberfill.

16 Lace up the bootie with the rattail cord.

17 Repeat steps 5 through 16 for the other bootie.

Spooky Friends Wall Hanging

DESIGNER: MOLLIE JOHANSON

Pssssst, these reverse appliquéd Halloween cuties think that they are a terrifying trio (so act afwaid, vewy, vewy afwaid).

WHAT YOU NEED

Basic sewing kit (page 9)

Templates (page 114)

Black felt, ¼ yard (22.9 cm)

One 6-inch (15.2 cm) felt square in each color: white, orange, gold, and purple

White, orange, purple, and black embroidery floss

Thin stick, about 11 inches (27.9 cm) long

¾-inch-wide (1.9 cm) orange fabric strip or ribbon, about 24 inches (61 cm) long

Scallop or pinking shears

WHAT YOU DO

1 Cut a 7 x 22-inch (17.8 x 55.9 cm) rectangle from the black felt. Set aside. Using the templates, cut the ghost square from black felt, the pumpkin square from gold felt, and the bat square from black felt. Cut out the center area from each square.

2 Center the ghost square on the white felt, the pumpkin square on the orange felt, and the bat square on the purple felt. Pin each shape, then stitch around the cutout opening only, using three strands of white, orange, or purple floss, and straight stitch.

3 Using the templates as a placement guide, embroider the faces in the cutout area of each square. Use three strands of black floss, French knots, and backstitch.

4 Cut around each of the outer squares with scallop or pinking shears. Pin the squares onto the large piece of black felt. Position them about ½ inch (1.3 cm) apart, leaving about 2½ inches (6.4 cm) at the top. Stitch the squares to the backing using three strands of coordinating floss and straight stitch.

5 Fold the top edge of the backing over to the back, then stitch across with straight stitch, creating a channel. Slide the stick through the channel, and tie the fabric or ribbon to each end for a hanger.

Felt-o-ween

Make this colorful skull garland using random bright colors,
a spectrum of rainbow colors, or—for a more gothic look—
blood red felt around each skull.

Rainbow Skull Garland

DESIGNER: LAURA HOWARD

WHAT YOU NEED

Basic sewing kit (page 9)

Templates (page 115)

2 white felt sheets, 9 x 12-inch (22.9 x 30.5 cm) each

Black felt, 6 x 8½ inches (15.2 x 21.6 cm)

9 bright colors of felt, 5½ x 9½ inches (14 x 24.1 cm) each

Matching sewing threads

Black embroidery floss

Black ribbon, approx. ⅝ inch (1.6 cm) wide and 8 feet (2.4 m) long

WHAT YOU DO

1 Use the templates provided to cut out the following felt pieces for each skull on your garland: one white skull, two black eyes, one black nose, and two bright backing shapes (both the same color).

2 Pin a skull shape in the center of one of the backing shapes. Use white sewing thread and straight stitches to sew around the edge of the skull onto the backing felt, and then remove the pins.

3 Pin the eyes and nose in position on the skull as pictured, and sew them in place with black sewing thread and more straight stitches. Then remove the pins.

4 Cut a length of black embroidery floss and split the strands. Switch to a larger needle if necessary, and use the floss to sew the skull's mouth. Backstitch three horizontal lines and then sew seven long vertical stitches between them to create two rows of teeth.

5 Repeat steps 2 through 4 for all the skulls.

6 Arrange the remaining backing shapes under a long piece of black ribbon a little over an inch (2.5 cm) below the top edge of the skull. Leave plenty of spare ribbon at each end so you can hang the garland, and leave a gap between each skull. Then pin the ribbon onto the backing shapes so that the ribbon will be sandwiched in between the front and back felt shapes when you join them together.

7 Sew the ribbon to the backing felt shapes, using whipstitch and taking care to sew into the felt but not through it. If you're not confident about doing this, use thread to match the backing felt. Otherwise, you can use any shade of thread. Then remove the pins.

8 Place the skulls on their corresponding backing shapes, and pin the layers together. Use whipstitches and matching thread to join the edges of each backing shape. Finish your stitching neatly at the back of each skull, and remove the pins. Then trim the ends of the ribbon at an angle to help prevent fraying.

Who doesn't want
a little vampire to
snuggle up with?

Vampire Plushie

WHAT YOU NEED

Basic sewing kit (page 9)

Templates (page 123)

Light gray felt, 7¾ x 10½ inches (19.7 x 26.7 cm)

White felt, 5 x 6¼ inches (12.7 x 15.9 cm)

Black felt, 7½ x 8¼ inches (19 x 21 cm)

Red felt, 3½ x 5¾ inches (8.9 x 14.6 cm)

Dark red felt, 5 x 5¼ inches (12.7 x 13.3 cm)

Matching sewing threads

Black and white embroidery floss

Fiberfill

Narrow black or dark red ribbon, 14 inches (35.6 cm) long

WHAT YOU DO

1 Use the templates provided to cut out the following felt pieces: two light gray vampire bodies, one black hair (front), one black hair (back), two black trousers, one black cape, one dark red cape, two white shirts, two white eyes, and one of each of the vest pieces in red. Cut two small black circles for pupils.

2 Add clothes to the vampire front and back. Pin the black trousers onto the body pieces, and use black sewing thread and whipstitch to sew them in place; then remove the pins.

Note: When adding the trousers, the other items of the vampire's clothing, and the hair (in a later step), just whipstitch the inner edges. The outer edges will be sewn up when the front and back of the vampire is sewn together later.

3 Pin the shirt in place, and sew it in position with white whipstitches. Remove the pins. Then add the vest pieces, pinning them in place so the front left piece slightly overlaps the right. Whipstitch them all in place with red sewing thread, and remove the pins.

4 Working on the front of the vampire only, cut a length of black embroidery floss and split the strands. Switch to a larger needle if necessary, and use the floss to sew a row of tiny stitches to create buttons on the waistcoat.

5 Pin the front and back hair shapes in position. Sew them in place with black sewing thread and whipstitches, and then remove the pins. Add the eyes to the vampire's face with white sewing thread and whipstitches. Pin and then stitch the black pupils in position with black whipstitches.

6 Use black embroidery floss to backstitch the vampire's smile. Then cut a length of white embroidery floss, split the strands, and sew the vampire's fangs. Create each fang by sewing two stitches to form a "V" shape and then filling that shape in with more small white stitches.

Tip: To help the white fangs and eyes stand out against the light gray felt, use black sewing thread to backstitch a line flush around the white shapes.

7 Pin the front and back of the vampire together, wrong sides together. Use light gray sewing thread and whipstitch around the edges. Start at the left where the head and arm meet, sew around the arm and the legs, and up to just under the right arm.

8 Stuff the left arm and the legs gradually. Then sew around the right arm with more light gray whipstitches, and stuff the right arm and the rest of the body. Continue sewing up around the head, stuffing gradually as you work. Finish your stitching neatly at the back.

9 Cut two lengths of narrow ribbon (black or dark red), each approximately 7 inches (17.8 cm). Use black sewing thread and whipstitches to sew a ribbon to each side of the black

cloak piece, where the pointed collar begins. Position each piece of ribbon so it overlaps the felt by about an inch (2.5 cm), and sew into the felt (not through it).

10 Pin the black and dark red cloak pieces together so the ribbon ends are sandwiched between them. Use black sewing thread to whipstitch the edges of the felt together. Finish your stitching neatly on the black side, and remove the pins.

11 Use the ribbons to tie the cloak around your vampire's neck, tying them in a bow. Trim the ribbons as desired, cutting the ends at an angle to help minimize fraying.

Devil-Made-Me-Do-It Pincushion

DESIGNER: LAURA HOWARD

Make this devilishly cute cushion for your needles, pins, and pitchforks.

WHAT YOU NEED

Basic sewing kit (page 9)

Templates (page 118)

**Dark gray or black felt, 6 x 10½ inches
(15.2 x 26.7 cm)**

Red felt, 2½ x 3½ inches (6.4 x 8.9 cm)

**Orange felt, 5½ x 9½ inches
(14 x 24.1 cm)**

**Light orange felt, 3½ x 4 inches
(8.9 x 10.2 cm)**

Yellow felt, 2 x 2½ inches (5 x 6.4 cm)

Matching sewing threads

Black and red embroidery floss

Fiberfill

WHAT YOU DO

1 Use the templates provided to cut out the following felt pieces: one dark gray circle, one orange circle (for the bottom), one red devil body, one red devil head, and one dark gray side piece. Trace the template for each flame layer, following the straight line along the bottom and the different lines (A, B & C) for each layer. Cut layer A from orange felt, layer B from light orange felt, and layer C from yellow felt. Also, cut out a small red triangle for the devil's tail.

2 Pin the devil's body on the gray circle, leaving room for the head. Sew the body in place with red whipstitches, and remove the pin. Then add the head and the triangle for the tail with more red thread and whipstitches. Remove the pin from the head if you've used one.

3 Cut a length of black embroidery floss and split the strands. Switch to a larger needle if necessary, and use the floss to sew the devil's eyes, mouth, and eyebrows. Sew three very small stitches close together for each eye, a single stitch for each eyebrow, and backstitch a curved line for the smile.

4 Cut a length of red embroidery floss, and separate half the strands. Use the floss to stitch the tail and pitchfork, using the photo as a guide. To sew the tail, start from the triangle and sew a curved line back to the body. To sew the pitchfork, sew a straight line and then sew a "U" shape at the top to form the other prongs of the fork.

5 Pin the orange flame piece (layer A) on the gray side piece so that the bottom edges line up and there's a small gap to the left of the flames. Sew the orange felt in place with whipstitches and matching sewing thread, leaving the bottom edge unstitched. Remove the pins.

6 Add the light orange flame pieces (layer B) one by one, pinning and then sewing them in place with matching thread and whipstitch. Remove the pins.

7 Add the yellow felt pieces (layer C) with yellow thread and more whipstitches. Leave the bottom edges unstitched, as before.

8 Hold the decorated top circle and the top left edge of the side piece together, wrong sides facing. Use matching thread and small whipstitches to sew the edges together, working counterclockwise around the circle and turning it gradually as you sew around it.

9 Trim any excess felt from the side piece—the two short edges should just slightly overlap—and join the edges together with a line of small straight stitches in matching thread.

10 Add the bottom circle with orange sewing thread and whipstitches, turning the circle as you sew around it. Leave a gap large enough to fit a couple of your fingers through. Stuff the pincushion gradually with small pieces of fiberfill until it's firmly and evenly stuffed. Then sew the final gap closed with more whipstitches, and finish your stitching neatly.

Tip: Adhere orange and yellow felt scraps to pins to make a set of flaming pins for your pincushion.

Graveyard Cupcake Toppers

DESIGNER: LAURA HOWARD

Decorate your cupcakes with cute little ghosts and creepy zombies rising from the grave…er, icing!

WHAT YOU NEED

Basic sewing kit (page 9)

Templates (page 115)

White felt, 4¾ x 7 inches (12.1 x 17.8 cm)

Gray felt, 3½ x 5 inches (8.9 x 12.7 cm)

Pale pink (or other skin color) felt, 3½ x 4 inches (8.9 x 10.2 cm)

Sewing thread in white, gray, black, red, and to match skin-tone

Black embroidery floss

Disappearing marker

Toothpicks

WHAT YOU DO

To Make the Ghosts

1 Use the template provided to cut out two white felt ghost pieces for each topper you want to make. If the felt you're using is quite thin or see-through, cut three pieces instead of two (see the tip below).

2 Cut a length of black embroidery floss and split the strands. Use a disappearing marker to draw a face on one of the ghost shapes; you can use the faces pictured as a guide, or create your own. Use backstitch for the mouth, and sew three or four very small stitches close together to create each eye.

Tip: If you're using thin felt, pin two ghost shapes together and stitch through both layers as you add the face. The added layer will make your finished ghost sturdier and also help prevent your knots from showing through.

3 Place the front of your ghost on another (un-decorated) ghost piece (wrong sides facing). Pin the pieces together, and use white sewing thread to sew a line of straight stitch around the edge, sewing the layers together. As you sew along the bottom edge, sew a long stitch in the center to create a gap large enough for inserting a toothpick. Finish your stitching neatly at the back, and remove the pin.

4 Repeat steps 1 through 3 for each ghost to create a whole set with different expressions.

To Make Each Gravestone

1 Use the template provided to cut out two gravestone shapes from gray felt.

2 Cut a length of black embroidery floss and split the strands. Use a disappearing marker to write RIP on the gravestone. Then use the floss to stitch over the letters, using small backstitches.

3 Place the decorated front and plain back gravestone shapes together (wrong sides facing) and pin them together. Sew a line of straight stitch around the edge with gray sewing thread, sewing a long stitch at the bottom center to create a gap for adding the toothpick. Finish your stitching neatly at the back, and remove the pin.

To Make Each Zombie Hand

1 Use the template provided to cut out one hand shape from pale pink felt. Embroidery scissors are great for cutting out small, fiddly shapes!

2 Sew a wound on the arm by backstitching a small line with red sewing thread. Then use black sewing thread to add a series of small single stitches across it.

3 Place the hand on a piece of matching pale pink felt, and sew the hand onto the backing felt with matching sewing thread and small straight stitches. Sew up one side of the hand, then sew up and down each finger with straight stitches, filling in the gaps between the stitching as you sew back down

and creating a continuous line of stitching along each finger. Then sew down the other side of the hand and along the bottom, sewing one long stitch to create a gap so you can add the toothpick. Finish your stitching neatly at the back.

4 Carefully cut around the hand shape (taking care not to cut through any of your stitching) to create a hand that's two layers of felt thick.

Tip: These toppers are designed so you can remove the toothpicks and reuse the toppers next year. (Feel free to lick off the icing!)

Quick, to the (super cute and handmade from felt) Bat Mobile!

Bat Mobile

DESIGNER: KATHY SHELDON

WHAT YOU NEED

Basic sewing kit (page 9)

Template (page 115)

4 to 6 black adhesive felt sheets, 9 x 12 inches (22.9 x 30.5 cm) each (see Note)

Freezer paper

1 skein of black floss (don't separate strands)

7-inch (17.8 cm) orange plastic embroidery hoop

Cotton ball (optional, see Tip)

Nail polish remover (optional, see Tip)

Note: If you use regular felt instead of the adhesive kind, you'll need to sew the two bat pieces together using black floss and a straight stitch around their outer edges.

WHAT YOU DO

1 Take two of the black adhesive felt sheets and carefully attach them, sticky sides together, to create a thick, double-sided sheet of black felt. Repeat with two more sheets. (Reserve the other two sheets in case you need them.)

2 Trace the bat template onto the non-waxy side of the freezer paper, cut it out roughly, and then iron it onto one side of the double-sided felt sheet. Use sharp curved manicure scissors or embroidery scissors to cut the bat shape out of the felt. Repeat to make eight more bats.

3 Cut the black floss to about 60 inches (1.5 m) in length, and knot it at one end. Using a large needle, sew two or three long stitches through the center of one bat (you'll have to poke fairly hard). Leave a few inches (5 cm) of floss, and stitch through another bat to add it. Leave a few more inches (5 cm), and stitch a third bat onto the strand. Remember to leave plenty of floss at the end for attaching to the hoop and hanging. Repeat this step to create two additional strands of bats.

Tip: Both the scissors used to cut the bats out and the needle used to stitch the floss through the bats will get sticky from the adhesive on the felt sheets. Clean them with a quick swipe from a cotton ball soaked in nail polish remover.

4 Wind the excess floss of one strand around the inner circle of the embroidery hoop, adjusting it so the strand hangs at the desired height. Knot the floss a couple of times to secure it in place, but don't trim the excess floss yet. Repeat this for the other two strands, knotting them in place equally spaced on the hoop.

5 Hold the hoop level, and carefully adjust the position of the bats so the arrangement is pleasing and balanced.

6 Hold the three floss ends in your hand, so the hoop hangs level. Tie all three strands together in one knot, leaving a loop at the top for hanging. Trim any excess floss.

These giant candies are nonfat, sugar free, and super sweet. What's not to love?

Trick or Treats

DESIGNER: CYNTHIA SHAFFER

WHAT YOU NEED

Basic sewing kit (page 9)

Templates (page 128)

FOR THE SWIRL LOLLIPOP

6-inch-square (15.2 cm) panel of white cardboard

Felt sheets (9 x 12 inches [22.9 x 30.5 cm]) in the following colors: 2 in white, 1 in orange, and 1 in red

White thread

Temporary spray adhesive

White glue

Paper swirl straw in red and white

Cellophane, 12 x 20 inches (30.5 x 50.8 cm)

Fishing line, 24 inches (61 cm) long

FOR THE GUMDROPS

Felt sheet in purple, bright pink, green, or yellow, 9 x 12 inches (22.9 x 30.5 cm)

Matching sewing thread

Fiberfill

Permanent spray adhesive

White glitter

FOR THE CANDY CORN

Felt sheets (9 x 12 inches [22.9 x 30.5 cm]) in the following colors: 2 in white, 1 in orange, and 1 in gold

Orange and gold thread

Fiberfill

FOR THE CANDY ROLL

Felt strips in light yellow, light orange, light pink, light green, and lavender, at least 6 inches (15.2 cm) long

White felt, 4¼ x 5¾ inches (10.8 x 14.6 cm)

Spray adhesive, temporary and permanent

Cardboard tube from a toilet paper roll

Newspaper

White cardstock scrap

Cellophane, 12 x 7 inches (30.5 x 17.8 cm)

Fishing line, 24 inches (61 cm) long

WHAT YOU DO

To Make the Swirl Lollipop

1 Trace lollipop template A onto the white cardboard, and cut out the shape.

2 Cut out two template A shapes from the white felt, one template B from the orange felt, and one template C from the red felt.

3 Arrange the orange and red swirls onto one of the white felt circles, and adhere them using the temporary spray adhesive.

4 Machine-stitch (or hand-stitch if you prefer) the swirls in place using a zigzag stitch and white thread.

5 Using the spray adhesive to adhere the layers, stack the stitched swirl circle on the white cardboard followed by the solid white felt circle.

6 Machine-stitch around the outer edge using a zigzag stitch. Leave a small opening unstitched at the bottom.

7 Gently lift up the white felt back at the unstitched opening, and fill the opening with a small amount of white glue.

8 Insert the straw and set it aside to dry.

9 Wrap the lollipop in the cellophane, and tie it with fishing line.

Felt-o-ween

49

To Make the Gumdrops

1 Trace template A onto one color of the felt four times and cut out the shapes.

2 Cut out one template B shape from the same color of felt.

3 Align two of the long edges of two template A felt pieces, and machine-stitch the edges together using a zigzag stitch. Repeat for the remaining two pieces.

4 Align these two pieces and machine-stitch the edges together using a zigzag stitch.

5 Fill the gumdrop with fiberfill.

6 Hand-stitch the bottom of the gumdrop to the top using an overcast stitch. When there are just 2 inches (5 cm) remaining to stitch, insert more fiberfill to puff out the bottom.

7 Lightly spray the gumdrop with spray adhesive and then roll in a pile of white glitter.

To Make the Candy Corn

1 Cut the following with the templates.

> A: cut 2 from the white felt
> B: cut 2 from the orange felt
> C: cut 2 from the gold felt
> D: cut 1 from the gold felt. Transfer side seam markings.

2 Stack the orange and gold felt onto the white felt, and zigzag stitch them in place with orange thread. Repeat for the other side.

3 With right sides together and with gold thread, machine-stitch around the candy corn along one side, up and over the top, and then down the other side. Stitch the seam using a ¼-inch (6 mm) seam allowance and a short stitch length. Back tack at the beginning and at the end.

4 Trim the seam close to the stitching.

5 Turn the candy corn right side out and stuff with fiberfill.

6 Using an overcast stitch and hand-sewing needle, stitch the bottom onto the candy corn, matching the side seam marks with the side seams. When there are just 2 inches (5 cm) remaining to sew closed, add extra fiberfill to help round out the bottom. Finish hand sewing the bottom to the candy corn.

To Make the Candy Roll

1 Arrange the thin strips of felt scraps on the white felt panel. Adhere the strips to the panel using the temporary spray adhesive.

2 Machine-stitch the strips in place using a zigzag stitch.

3 Stuff the cardboard tube with newspaper until it feels like the sides of the tube are strong and resist a squeeze.

4 Trace template A twice onto the cardstock and twice onto the felt scraps. The felt circles should be cut from the same color as the end candies. Cut out the circles.

5 Spray the cardstock circles with the permanent spray adhesive and then press them onto the ends of the filled tube.

6 Spray the backside of the stitched white felt panel with permanent spray adhesive, and adhere it to the tube. If the felt panel is a little too long, trim off the excess before you wrap it completely around the tube.

7 Using permanent spray adhesive, spray the felt circles and adhere them to the ends of the tube, onto the cardstock circles.

8 Wrap the roll in cellophane and twist the ends, and then tie them with a length of fishing line.

9 Trim the ends of the cellophane, if needed.

Ears-to-You Headbands

DESIGNER: LAURA HOWARD

All it takes is some scraps
of felt, a few stitches, and
a purchased headband
to make these whimsical
animal ears.

WHAT YOU NEED

Basic sewing kit (page 9)

Templates (page 110)

**Felt for outer ears, up to
6½ x 7½ inches (16.5 x 19 cm)**

**Felt for inner ears, up to
3 x 3½ inches (7.6 x 8.9 cm)**

Matching sewing threads

Plastic headband

Craft glue (optional)

**Note: For best results, use felt that
is stiff or thicker than standard craft
felt. The amount of felt needed varies between headbands. The amount
listed above is what you'll need for
the largest set (the rabbit ears).**

WHAT YOU DO

1 Use the templates provided to cut out two outer ear shapes and two inner ear shapes in the required felt colors for your chosen animal. If you're using a headband that's very wide or narrow, you may need to alter the templates slightly by increasing or decreasing the space between the dotted lines: this is the section that wraps around the headband.

2 Position one of the inner ear shapes on one of the outer ear shapes. Pin the inner shape in place, and secure it with whipstitches in matching sewing thread around the edges. Remove the pin. Then repeat this step for the second ear so you have two matching ears.

3 Fold one of the ears around the headband (right sides out) so that the top edges of the ear line up, then pin the ear together at the top. Make sure the ear is in the position you want, then pull the felt tightly around the curve of the headband and hold it in place.

Tip: If your headband has teeth (like the bands pictured), these should be enough to help hold the felt ears in place when they're sewn together. If not, add some craft glue to the underside of the headband before wrapping the felt ear around it.

4 Use matching sewing thread to sew a line of straight stitch flush with the top edge of the headband, sewing the front and back of the ear together so the felt is wrapped tightly around the band. Then remove the pin.

5 Whipstitch around the edge of the ear, sewing the sides together with matching thread. Finish your stitching neatly at the back. The felt ear may now have curved slightly; shape it so it curves out at the front.

6 Repeat steps 3 through 5 for the second ear.

Note: If you're making the rabbit ears, cut two extra inner ear shapes from white felt. Insert one of these extra pieces in between the front and back of each of the rabbit's ears after step 4 to help support them.

Elegantly evil, these
felt roses will add
just the right touch
of dark glam to your
Halloween décor.

Darkling Roses

DESIGNER: KATHY SHELDON

WHAT YOU NEED

TO MAKE ONE

Basic sewing kit (page 9)

Template (page 119)

Black felt sheet, 9 x 12 inches (22.9 x 30.5 cm)

Black pipe cleaners

Hot glue gun and glue or fabric glue

Black thread

Wire cutters or craft scissors

Note: One felt sheet is enough for two roses and two leaves.

WHAT YOU DO

1 Use the template to cut one circle for each rose you want to make. You don't really need to trace the spiral pattern that's on the template—just cut it freehand. Leave a small circular shape at the center of each spiral you cut.

2 Snip a small slit into the circular shape at the end of your cut spiral strip; it only needs to be big enough to poke a pipe cleaner through, but don't poke it through yet.

3 Starting with the outermost end of the spiral, roll the strip of felt around itself, tighter at first and then a bit looser as you get to the end of the strip. Leave the small circular bit of felt at the end hanging loose for now. Hold the base of the rose securely, and shape the rose petals as desired.

Tip: Don't get frustrated if your first couple of rolling attempts are awkward or if the felt doesn't look like a rose when you start rolling. Once you get the hang of this, it's super easy, and the rose will "bloom" as you continue rolling.

4 Still holding the base of the rose securely, insert one end of a black pipe cleaner through the back of the slit in the small circle of felt and then into the center of the back of the rose. Poke it in far enough to be secure, but not so far that it pokes out the front of the rose.

5 Add hot glue or fabric glue to the base of the rose and surrounding the pipe cleaner. Press the small circle of felt snug against the base of the rose. Set the rose aside to dry.

6 Fold a scrap of black felt in half, and using the leaf template, cut one long leaf shape. Cut a very small vertical slit in the folded edge of the leaf.

7 Use the wire cutters (or craft scissors, but not your good fabric shears!) to cut a 3-inch (7.6 cm) length of black pipe cleaner.

8 Poke a couple of inches of the short pipe cleaner through the slit and into the leaf. Starting at one side of the leaf base, use the black thread and the straight stitch to stitch around the outer edge, sewing the front and back of the leaf together with the pipe cleaner sandwiched in between. When you get to the opposite edge of the leaf base, take a few stitches back and forth to the other side to secure the leaf to the pipe cleaner. Knot your thread.

9 Twist the open end of the pipe cleaner around the rose's pipe cleaner stem a couple of times. Bend the leaf to the shape desired. Repeat steps 2 through 9 for each rose.

Monster Hands

DESIGNER: AMANDA CARESTIO

*Give a monster-sized handshake with a set of spooky hands!
Don't worry: wrist straps keep your hands free for candy-grabbing fun.*

WHAT YOU NEED

Basic sewing kit (page 9)

Templates (page 119)

**Sheet of felt in dark gray and tan,
9 x 12 inches (22.9 x 30.5 cm)**

**4 green felt sheets, 9 x 12 inches
(22.9 x 30.5 cm)**

Marker

Fiberfill

Hook-and-loop tape (optional)

WHAT YOU DO

1 Use the templates to cut eight nails from dark gray felt. Cut 10 rough circles from tan felt, the wonkier the better.

2 Transfer and cut out the hand template. Stack two of the green felt sheets together, pin the template in place on top, and trace around the hand template, adding ¼ inch (6 mm) around all the edges.

3 While the sheets are still stacked, from one of the corners, cut two ½ x 5-inch (1.3 x 12.7 cm) strips (four strips total since the felt is double) for wrist straps.

4 Working on the top layer of green felt only, arrange five tan circles within the traced hand shape, and stitch them in place.

5 On the bottom layer, stitch the strips (from step 3) in place, using the placement marks on the template as a guide.

Tip: For a custom fit, cut the wrist strap in half and attach hook-and-loop tape to each cut end.

6 With the top layer face up and the bottom layer face down, stack and pin the green layers back together and stitch around the outside edge, working just inside your traced lines and leaving the bottom straight edge unstitched.

7 Cut around the hand, cutting through both layers and as close to the stitched seam as possible.

8 Fold the nail shapes in half and pin them in place on the fingertips. Stitch them in place along one angled edge and then along the other. If the felt has shifted, trim the edges to straighten them.

9 Stuff the hand so the fingers are quite full and firm. Only partially stuff the wrists.

10 Stitch along the bottom open edge.

11 Repeat for the other hand, reversing the hand template in step 2.

Silly Scarecrow Plant Picks

DESIGNER: MOLLIE JOHANSON

WHAT YOU NEED

Basic sewing kit (page 9)

Templates (page 115)

Rust felt, about 3½ x 4½ inches (8.9 x 11.4 cm)

Gold felt, about 3½ x 4½ inches (8.9 x 11.4 cm)

Tan felt, about 1 x 2 inches (2.5 x 5 cm)

Charcoal gray felt, about 3 x 3½ inches (7.6 x 8.9 cm)

Orange and black embroidery floss

Scraps of natural twisted paper ribbon or brown craft paper

Fabric glue

2 wooden skewers

Glue gun and glue stick

WHAT YOU DO

1 Using the templates, cut two hats and two pairs of pants from the rust felt, two shirts and one beak from the gold felt, two heads from the tan felt, and two crows from the charcoal gray felt.

2 Embroider the scarecrow face onto one head shape, using three strands of black floss, French knots, and backstitch. Stitch two lines of straight stitch on one hat, one shirt (across both sleeves and the bottom edge), and one pair of pants using three strands of orange floss.

3 Stitch the crow's eyes with French knots and his feather details with straight stitch using three strands of black floss.

4 Untwist the paper ribbon, and cut a strip that is about ¾ inch (1.9 cm) wide. Fringe one side, then cut lengths of fringe to fit the scarecrow's hat, sleeves, shirt bottom, and pant legs. You may need to cut and overlap two pieces for the bottom of the shirt.

5 Glue the two pants pieces together using fabric glue, placing the fringed "straw" between the layers. Glue the two shirt pieces together with the pants and "straw" between the layers. Glue the two layers of the head together, then glue the head to the front of the shirt. Glue the two hat pieces together with the top of the head and the "straw" between the layers.

6 Glue the crow's beak in place, and glue the two body pieces together using fabric glue.

7 After the glue has thoroughly dried, attach the skewers to the back of the scarecrow and crow with a line of hot glue.

Add some harvest charm to a pot of mums
with this scarecrow and his buddy.

Got a collection of those reusable cloth grocery bags? Just turn them inside out and use adhesive felt to create fast, no-sew trick-or-treat bags.

Monster Sugar Stash Bags

DESIGNER: SUZIE MILLIONS

WHAT YOU NEED

Templates (pages 124-125)

3 black shopping bags, 12 inches (30.5 cm) square

White, hot pink, and bright green felt, 13-inch (33 cm) squares

Black self-adhesive felt, two 9 x 12-inch (22.9 x 30.5 cm) sheets

White self-adhesive felt, 4 inches (10.2 cm) square

Bright yellow felt, two 2½ x 2-inch (6.4 x 5 cm) pieces

Dark, medium, and light gray felt, one 9 x 12-inch (22.9 x 30.5 cm) sheet of each

Ultra-hold iron-on adhesive

Medium-point permanent marker

Iron

Parchment paper (optional)

Craft knife

Note: Turn your reusable shopping bag wrong side out so the outsides are plain.

WHAT YOU DO

1 Smooth out a sheet of iron-on adhesive, paper side up. Align the face template ¼ inch (6 mm) in from the edges, and draw a line around it with the marker. Cut the shape out from the sheet ¼ inch (6 mm) beyond the outline of the template. Follow the product directions for bonding the adhesive to one of the 13-inch-square (33 cm) felt pieces, cut the felt, and then iron the felt piece to a bag. Repeat with the other two bags.

Tip: If you're using a repurposed, non-fabric bag, put parchment over the felt piece when you iron to avoid melting the bag.

2 For Psycha-Skullic and Franken-Fill-Me-Up bags, trace the template pieces onto the back of the self-adhesive felt, cut them out, and stick the pieces in place using the photos as a guide.

3 For Mummy-Can-I-Have-More-Candy, trace the templates for the gray pieces onto scraps of iron-on adhesive. Follow the product directions for bonding those pieces of adhesive to the gray felt. Cut them out, and iron on all the gray pieces except the nose. Peel the backing off the black piece that goes around the eyes. Position the scraps of yellow felt behind the eyeholes, and then press them in place on the back. Add the rest of the black and white self-adhesive piece. Iron on the nose last.

Inspired by a vintage Halloween card, this brooch is just the thing to brighten a cardigan in October.

Cat in Pumpkin Brooch

DESIGNER: KATHY SHELDON

WHAT YOU NEED

Basic sewing kit (page 9)

Templates (page 120)

Freezer paper (for transferring the templates)

Olive green, gray, black, and orange wool felt

Olive green, black, orange, and gray floss

Metal pinback

Small piece of thin cardboard or cardstock

WHAT YOU DO

1 Trace each template onto the smooth (non-waxy) side of a piece of freezer paper, tracing two large ovals, two pumpkin eyes, and one of the other shapes. Cut around each shape roughly, leaving a small border of the freezer paper.

2 Iron the two large oval templates onto the olive green felt; the small oval onto the gray felt; the cat, the two pumpkin eyes, the pumpkin nose, and the pumpkin mouth onto the black felt; and the pumpkin onto the orange felt.

3 Cut each shape out carefully, and remove the freezer paper.

4 Using the photo for reference, position the pumpkin onto the gray felt, and use the straight stitch and the orange floss to attach it, emphasizing the cut top of the pumpkin and the pumpkin ribs.

5 Position the eyes, nose, and mouth on the pumpkin. Use the straight stitch and the black floss to attach each piece.

6 Position the cat "inside" the pumpkin top. Use the straight stitch and black floss to attach the cat to the gray felt.

7 Make a few horizontal stitches with the orange floss for the eyes. Make one vertical stitch across the middle of each eye with the black floss. Use black floss and tiny stitches to make the cat's nose.

8 Thread a needle with three strands of gray floss, and insert the needle from the front to the back at one side of the cat's nose. Pull a little floss through and then make a knot in the floss in the back, catching a bit of the felt. Poke the needle back through so it comes out at the front on the other side of the nose. Clip both sides of the floss in the front to create the cat's whiskers.

9 Use the black floss and the straight stitch to attach the gray felt oval to the front of one large green oval of felt.

10 Use the olive green floss to sew the pinback just above center on the back of the plain green oval.

11 Use the small oval template to cut an oval from the thin cardboard or cardstock. Sandwich the cardstock oval between the two large green ovals.

12 Use the green floss and the blanket stitch to attach the two ovals together at their outer edges.

Haunted House Candy Bag

DESIGNER: JODIE RACKLEY

This trick-or-treat bag, made with simple embroidery stitches and two layers for added strength, will add one-of-a-kind charm to your child's Halloween adventures!

WHAT YOU NEED

Basic sewing kit (page 9)

Templates (page 126)

½ yard (45.7 cm) of purple felt

Gray felt sheet, 9 x 12 inches (22.9 x 30.5 cm)

Scraps of felt in various colors for the appliqués

Tissue paper

Embroidery floss in purple and various colors to match the appliqués

2 lengths of super jumbo rickrack, at least 8 inches (20.3 cm) each

WHAT YOU DO

1 Using the full house template, cut out four pieces from the purple felt: two for the front and two for the back. Cut one roof piece from the gray felt. Cut two shutters and a strip measuring 2 to 3 inches (5 to 7.6 cm) wide by 25 inches (63.5 cm) long from the purple felt.

2 Use the templates to cut two window squares, the ghost, door, door windows, pumpkin, and bat from scraps of felt. Free-hand cut two small triangles and one thin strip for the pumpkin face, one small triangle for the pumpkin stem, three skinny rectangles for the skull door, and two small circles for the wicked flowers.

3 Trace the roof template with the tiles onto the piece of tissue paper. Place the gray roof shape onto the top of one of the full house pieces. Line up the tissue paper tracing with the gray roof shape, and layer both on top of one of the purple house shapes.

4 Using purple floss, backstitch along the traced line through the two layers of felt, leaving the sides and top of the roof un-stitched; we'll get to those later. Once you have stitched all but the outside lines of the roof, gently tug at the tissue paper to remove it from the stitches and reveal the stitched roof design.

5 Pin the main skull door piece in the bottom center of the house, leaving a bit of room on the bottom so you can stitch around it later. Pin the ghost in place behind the edge of the door. Stitch around the outside edge of the door using matching floss, making

sure to stitch through the "tail" of the ghost. Use the straight stitch and matching floss to stitch around the outside edge of the ghost. Position the two windowpanes and the three small rectangles on the skull, and stitch them in place using matching floss. Use satin stitches to create nostrils.

6 Stitch the ghost's face, using two small cross stitches of fuchsia floss for eyes and satin stitch to form the oval for its mouth.

7 Pin the pumpkin and stem shapes to the left of the skull door in place. Using matching floss, sew a straight stitch around the edge of the pumpkin, making sure to stitch through the triangle stem when you go around the top. Pin and then stitch in place the pumpkin eyes and mouth.

Tip: Use a little dab of felt glue instead of stitching the small appliqué pieces, if you'd like.

8 Place the two small circles for the flowers beneath the ghost. Tack them in place with a few small random appliqué stitches to resemble spiky flowers. Using the green floss, make a couple of backstitches on the bottom, and use several straight stitches or satin stitch to form some leaves.

9 Pin the two window squares and shutters above the door, and stitch them in place using the backstitch and purple floss. Stitch around the sides of the shutters and then add some random stitches in the center of the shutters to add a bit of interest.

10 Position the bat shape so it overlaps the window on the left a bit, centering the body first and then placing the wings underneath so that the body overlaps them. Stitch the body down first using small straight stitches, and then do the same for the wings. Use another color of floss to make two small straight stitches for the bat's eyes.

11 To construct the bag, layer and pin the appliquéd front onto one of the remaining purple house shapes. Layer the two remaining house pieces, and pin those together. Working along the top short edge, sandwich the ends of the rickrack between the two felt layers. Starting at the bottom side of the roof, backstitch along the edge of the roof shape to finishing forming the lines on the roof, stitching the ends of the bag straps in place between the layers. Repeat this step for the backside of the bag, working the backstitch along the top of the bag where the roof is and securing the rickrack strap between the layers.

12 Starting with the front of the bag, pin the edge of the long purple strip (from step 1) along the side and bottom edge of the bag so that it goes all the way around and meets the other side at the bottom of the roof. Whipstitch all the way around the edge, closing the sides and bottom of the bag.

13 Flip the bag over, place the back on, and repeat step 12. Knot and tie off the thread on the inside of the bag. Your trick-or-treat bag is ready to go to a party or be filled with candy!

Pumpkin Patch Players

DESIGNER: SUZIE MILLIONS

Invite this lively band to your Halloween
shindig for a pickin' and grinnin' good time.

WHAT YOU NEED

TO MAKE THE WHOLE SET

Basic sewing kit (page 9)

Templates (page 111)

Glue stick

Felt sheets, 9 x 12 inches (22.9 x 30.5 cm) as follows: 3 in purple, 2 in orange, 2 in pink, and 1 in green

3 small yogurt containers (empty and cleaned)

Three 3-inch (7.6 cm) plastic foam balls

Chenille stems, 2 green and 6 orange

Felt scraps in white and yellow

2 drink stirrers

Gold cord or heavy thread (for strings)

Large-eye hand-sewing needle

20 white sequins

Scrap paper

Tacky craft glue

Craft knife

WHAT YOU DO

1 Copy the template. Apply glue stick to the entire printed side of the body template. Press it onto a piece of purple felt. Cut out the shape using the template, quickly remove the template from the felt, and use it to cut out two additional body pieces.

Tip: You'll use this same technique to transfer and cut out the rest of the template pieces needed for this project.

2 Apply a bead of tacky glue across the top of the body piece, ¼ inch (6 mm) down from the top edge (the straight notch on the lower hem should be on your right). Starting on the side with the straight notch, wrap the body piece around the yogurt container. The top of the "teeth" should extend past the edge of the container. Apply a thin bead of glue to the overlapping edge, and press it down gently. Repeat for the other two yogurt containers.

3 Using the templates, for each head, cut six head panels from the bright pink felt. After removing the templates, place the panels aside on scrap paper, glued side facing up.

4 One at a time, add glue to the edges of the pink panels and press them onto one of the foam balls, spacing them evenly around the ball (envision a clock here!).

5 Repeat steps 3 and 4 using the orange felt. When you place the orange panels, center them over the gaps between the pink panels.

6 Cut a bright green chenille stem in half to make two 6-inch (15.2 cm) pieces. Fold each piece in half. Insert one end (the loose end) into the top center of one of the foam balls. Push about half of it into the foam, and gently curve the half sticking out to resemble a pumpkin stem.

7 Using the templates, cut out the pieces for the instruments. In addition to the template pieces, you'll need the following parts: two ¾-inch (1.9 cm) lengths of drink stirrer (for the fiddle's tuning pegs), a 1½-inch (3.8 cm) piece of drink stirrer (for the bass fiddle stand), and two very thin strips of purple felt, 1½ inches (3.8 cm) long (for the bass fiddle F-holes). Assemble each instrument using the photo as a guide. Stitch the strings after all

three instruments are assembled, stitching from the back to the front and making a knot before and after each stitch. To make the fiddle bow, thread gold cord through a drink stirrer and tie the ends together.

8 Create the arms. With the seam at the back, push the tip of the craft knife blade through the covered yogurt container, ½ inch (1.3 cm) down from the top edge, twice to create a tiny "X" shape. Repeat again on the other side of the body (about 2 inches [5 cm] away from the first hole). Push an orange chenille stem through each hole. Pull up 2 inches (5 cm) above the rim, and twist the ends together to join them securely. Tug on each arm to pull the joint down inside the body.

9 Bend each chenille stem arm 2 inches (5 cm) out to make an elbow. On each arm,

make two bends 3½ inches (8.9 cm) up from the elbow; a 1¼-inch (3.2 cm) deep bend for the hand and a 1-inch (2.5 cm) bend for the thumb. Wrap the remainder of the chenille stem tightly around the base of the bends to finish the mitten. For each musician, bend and press the left hands to hold the instrument, and then arrange the right hands to play them.

10 Using the templates, cut out the noses and pupils for the eyes from scraps of yellow and purple felt. From purple felt, create the mouths by cutting very thin strips from a 2-inch (5 cm) square. Position each head so that the very bottom is not visible, and so that the eyes can be glued on orange strips and the nose on pink. Vary each character slightly to give them their own personality.

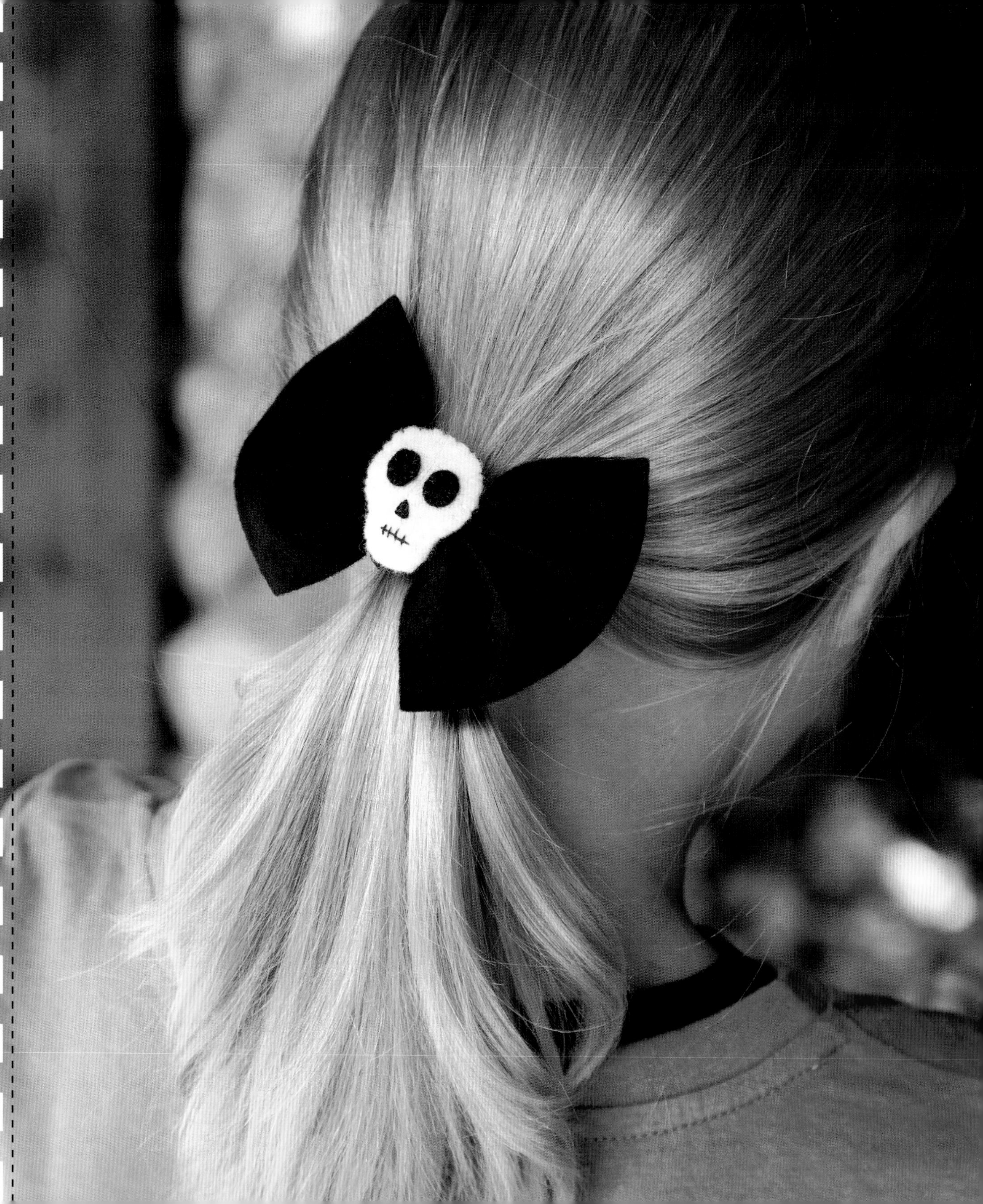

Skull Hairbows

DESIGNER: LAURA HOWARD

We love the mix of cute and ghoulish in these felt skull hairbows!

WHAT YOU NEED

TO MAKE ONE

Basic sewing kit (page 9)

Templates (page 113)

White felt, 1½ x 2½ inches (3.8 x 6.4 cm)

Dark felt (for bow), 4½ x 4¾ inches (11.4 x 12.1 cm)

A scrap of black felt

Matching sewing threads

Black embroidery floss

Black hair tie

WHAT YOU DO

1 Use the templates provided to cut out two skulls from white felt, two eyes from black felt, and one of each bow piece (A, B, and C) from your chosen dark felt.

2 Sew the two eye shapes onto one of the skull shapes using whipstitch and black sewing thread. Then use a double thickness of the black thread to sew the skull's mouth: backstitch a horizontal line and then sew four small vertical stitches along the line.

3 Cut a length of black embroidery floss and split the strands. Switch to a larger needle if necessary, and sew three small stitches to form a triangle for the skull's nose. Then fill in the triangle with more small black stitches.

4 Arrange bow piece C and the second skull shape so the skull is in the center of the rectangle, with the ends of the rectangle sticking out from the top and bottom of the skull. Use white sewing thread to sew the skull to the strip of dark felt, sewing a few overlapping stitches in the center of the skull.

5 Take the front (decorated) skull piece and place it on top of the back skull piece. Use whipstitches and more white sewing thread to sew the two skull pieces together, taking care not to sew through the dark felt behind the skull.

6 Fold bow piece A seven times along its length to create a concertina or accordion shape. Try to make each folded section approximately the same size to give your bow an even shape. Hold the folded felt together with your fingers, and use matching sewing thread to sew through the folds in the center several times, creating the bow shape.

7 Position an elastic hair tie at the back of the bow where you want it, and hold the tie and bow together. You will need to sew through the hair tie to help secure it, so if your hair tie

has a metal section, make sure this is positioned away from the felt bow. Wrap bow piece B around the middle of the bow and the hair tie, so the strip of felt holds the tie and bow together.

8 Secure the overlapping narrow end of bow piece B with whipstitches in matching sewing thread. Then sew through (or into) the hair tie a few times where it's wrapped in the felt, and sew through the center of the felt bow a few times as well to make sure all the pieces are securely attached to each other.

9 Position bow piece C so that the skull is in the center of the bow, and wrap the strip around the bow so the ends overlap at the back. Sew the overlapping end in place with whipstitch in matching thread, and then sew through the center of the bow a few times so piece C (and the attached skull) can't twist out of position. Finish your stitching neatly at the back of the bow.

Tip: Try these felt bows on an elastic headband, French barrette backs, or bobby pins for even more tress-taming options.

Sew Gross Hand Warmers

DESIGNER: KATHY SHELDON

Stitch up these rice-filled body parts, pop them in the microwave for 20 seconds, and tuck them in your little one's pockets for some yucky warmth on Halloween night.

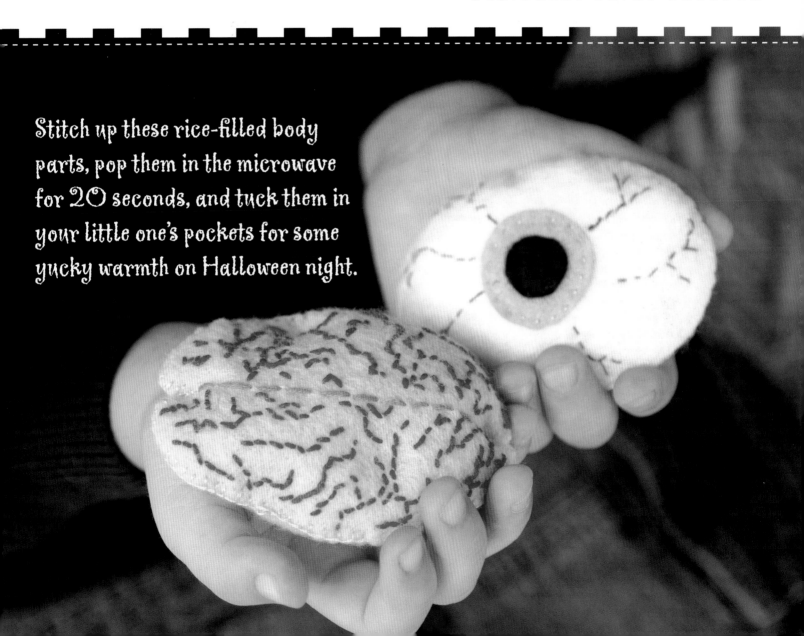

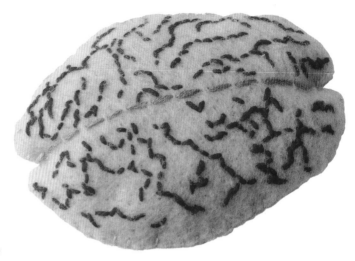

WHAT YOU NEED

Basic sewing kit (page 9)

Templates (page 116)

Several tablespoons of rice

FOR THE BRAIN

Light pink wool felt (see Note)

Dark pink, red, and light pink embroidery floss

FOR THE SEVERED FINGER

Tan, cream, and red wool felt

Dark brown, cream, tan, and red embroidery floss

FOR THE EYEBALL

White, light blue, and black wool felt

Black, light blue, and red embroidery floss

Note: Use wool felt for this project so you can safely warm the items in a microwave.

WHAT YOU DO

To Make the Brain

1 Trace the template onto tissue paper, cut around the template roughly, and pin the tissue paper to the pink felt.

2 Stitching right through the tissue paper, use long straight stitches and the dark pink floss to embroider the line down the center of the brain. Use short straight stitches and the red floss to embroider all the squiggly lines on the brain.

3 Carefully cut the brain shape out from the pink felt. Tear away the tissue paper, removing any stuck bits with your needle or tweezers.

4 Use the template to cut a second brain shape from the pink felt. Place it under the embroidered brain piece.

5 Use the blanket stitch and the light pink floss to sew around the outside edge of the brain, leaving a small opening.

6 Fill the brain with rice, and then finish stitching, hiding the knot on the inside.

To Make the Severed Finger

1 Use the tissue paper method (steps 1 through 3 for the brain) to stitch the finger details (with dark brown floss and straight stitches), and then cut the finger shape out of tan felt.

2 Use the template to cut a second finger shape from the tan felt, the fingernail from the cream felt, and the bottom from the red felt.

3 Use straight stitches and the cream floss to attach the fingernail to the tip of the embroidered finger.

4 Place the plain finger piece under the embroidered finger piece, and starting at one bottom corner, stitch around to the other bottom corner.

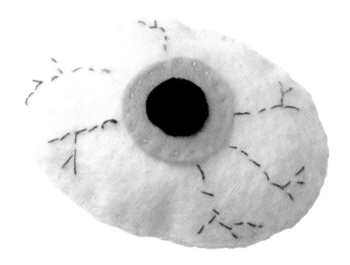

5 Use the red floss and intentionally sloppy slipstitches to attach the red bottom to the bottom of the finger, leaving a small opening.

6 Fill the finger with rice, and then finish stitching, hiding the knot on the inside.

To Make the Eyeball

1 Use the templates to cut a small circle from the black felt, a larger circle from the light blue felt, and two large ovals from the white felt.

2 Use the black floss and small straight stitches to attach the black circle to the center of the light blue circle.

3 Use the light blue floss and small straight stitches to attach the light blue circle to the center of the white oval.

4 Use the red floss and intentionally sloppy straight stitches to add veins to the eyeball, using the template stitch lines as a guide.

5 Place the plain white oval behind the embellished one. Use the white floss and the blanket stitch to attach the two pieces around the outside edge, leaving a small opening.

6 Fill with rice and then finish stitching, hiding the knot on the inside.

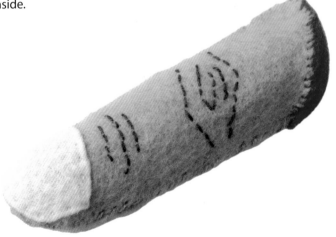

Pumpkin Napkins

DESIGNER: CYNTHIA SHAFFER

These napkins (which can be used for Halloween and Thanksgiving) may be too cute to wipe your mouth with. Best served with a slice of pumpkin pie!

WHAT YOU NEED

Basic sewing kit (page 9)

Templates (page 110)

Felt scraps in orange, gold, rust, and green

Temporary spray adhesive

Perle cotton floss in black, orange, white, and green

Cloth napkins in orange, yellow, and black

WHAT YOU DO

1 Cut out pumpkin shapes using templates A, B, C, D, E, and F from the orange, gold, and rust felt. Cut out pumpkin stems using template G and the green felt.

2 Use the temporary spray adhesive to adhere the pumpkins to the napkins. Stack the smaller pumpkins on top of the larger pumpkins.

3 Hand-stitch around the smaller and larger pumpkin shapes with a blanket stitch. Use the black floss on both the orange and the yellow napkin, and use white floss on the black napkin.

4 Using orange or white floss, create an additional set of contour lines on each smaller pumpkin shape.

5 Hand-stitch the stems in place above the pumpkins with a blanket stitch and green floss.

6 Hand-stitch tendrils near the stems, using a backstitch in black or white floss.

7 Lightly press the backs of the napkins.

Day of the Dead Kid's Tee

DESIGNER: CYNTHIA SHAFFER

You know that bag of felt scraps you've been saving?
Stitch them up into this festive El Día de los Muertos tee.

WHAT YOU NEED

Basic sewing kit (page 9)

Templates (page 117)

White felt sheet, 9 x 12 inches
(22.9 x 30.5 cm)

Felt scraps in orange, gold, lime green,
purple, turquoise, fuchsia, and black

Temporary spray adhesive

Black and white floss

Large-eye embroidery needle

Purple T-shirt (Note: The project shown
was made in girls' size 7/8.)

WHAT YOU DO

1 Cut your template pieces as follows:

A: one from white felt

B: one from orange felt

C: two from gold felt

D: one from white felt

E: two from lime green felt

F: two from turquoise felt

G: one from black felt

H: three from lime green felt
and three from fuchsia felt

I: one from fuchsia felt

J: three from lime green felt
and two from purple felt

K: two from black felt
and two from purple felt

L: two from orange felt

2 Using the photo for reference, use temporary spray adhesive to adhere the felt pieces to the T-shirt, centered on the front.

3 Hand-stitch all the pieces in place with the blanket stitch (page 12). Stitch with black floss for all the pieces except the black nose-piece cut from template G; stitch this piece with white floss.

4 Stitch across the mouthpiece (template D) with long straight stitches (page 13) to simulate teeth.

5 Stitch Xs to the face, under the left eye, at the left temple, and above the right eye.

Tip: Turn inside out and use cold water to wash.

· Felt-o-ween

80

Undead doesn't have to mean uncool. Whether you're going for bloody or stitched up, it's important to accessorize.

Undead Chokers & Bracelets

DESIGNER: KATHY SHELDON

WHAT YOU NEED

Basic sewing kit (page 9)

Templates (page 113)

Freezer paper (for transferring the templates)

Black felt

Red felt

1 small sew-on snap for each piece

Black thread

Red thread

WHAT YOU DO

1 Use the templates to trace the choker or bracelet onto the smooth (non-waxy) side of freezer paper.

2 Cut around the shape roughly, leaving a small border of the freezer paper.

3 Iron the freezer paper (waxy side down) onto the black or red felt. Cut out the shape carefully, and then remove the freezer paper.

4 Place the piece around your neck or wrist to determine the length needed, and then cut any excess if necessary.

5 Sew one side of the snap to the front of one end of the piece and the other side of the snap to the back of the other end.

Felt-o-ween

What's better than a festive bunting? How about
one that doesn't require a single stitch!

No-Sew Halloween Bunting

DESIGNER: STEPHANIE LYNN LIEBERT

WHAT YOU NEED

Basic sewing kit (page 9)

Templates (page 127)

Black and orange felt

Fabric (various coordinating patterns)

Fusible bonding tape

Black double-fold bias tape

WHAT YOU DO

1 Use the templates to cut nine large triangles from the black felt, nine medium triangles from the orange felt, and nine small triangles from the patterned fabric. (Use more or fewer pennants for your bunting, depending on the length desired—the one shown is about 68 inches [1.7 m] long.)

2 Outline the back of one small fabric triangle with strips of the fusible bonding tape. Carefully flip the fabric triangle over so it is centered on one orange felt triangle, and iron it in place following the manufacturer's directions. It usually does not take more than 30 seconds for the materials to fuse. Keep the iron moving, especially with the felt since felt fibers will melt if the iron is left in one spot for too long. Repeat for all fabric and orange felt triangles.

3 Once all of the fabric triangles have been bonded to the orange felt pieces, bond each of those pairs to a black felt triangle, using the fusible bonding tape method in the previous step.

4 Complete the bunting by sandwiching the top edges of the triangles inside the black double-fold bias tape. To do so, open the bias tape and lay out the felt triangles, spacing them evenly along the tape. Layer a piece of bonding tape along the front and back top edges of the triangles, then re-fold the bias tape over the edges and iron to secure.

Snotty Monster Soap Dispenser

DESIGNER: KATHY SHELDON

Hand washing is disgustingly fun with this little monster. Add green soap to your dispenser to enhance the...ah-choo!...gross-out factor.

WHAT YOU NEED

Basic sewing kit (page 9)

Templates (page 123)

Freezer paper

Liquid soap dispenser with purple nozzle

2 purple felt sheets, 9 x 12 inches (22.9 x 30.5 cm)

White and lime green felt scraps

Black embroidery floss

White, lime green, and purple thread

WHAT YOU DO

1 Use the templates to trace the monster head, body, and eyes onto the smooth (non-waxy) side of freezer paper twice. Transfer the line for the nose slit onto one head tracing. Trace each of the polka dot circles once.

Note: You may need to adjust the template to fit your soap dispenser. If you do so, make sure the slit for the monster's nozzle nose falls in the right place.

2 Cut around each shape roughly, leaving a small border of the freezer paper.

3 Iron the two monster heads and bodies onto the purple felt. Iron the two eyes onto the white felt. Iron the polka dot circles onto the lime green felt. Cut each shape out carefully, and remove the freezer paper except for the head shape with the line for the nose slit.

4 Hold the monster head that still has the freezer paper attached up to your soap dispenser to make sure the line for the nose slit is in the correct position. Adjust the location if necessary.

5 Cut the nose slit (erring on the side of making it too small), and remove the freezer paper. Carefully poke the soap dispenser's nozzle through the slit, cutting the slit larger if necessary, but make sure to cut evenly so the slit stays centered in the face.

6 Using the photo for reference, place the two eye circles onto the purple head with the nose slit, and use all six strands of the black floss to make a large French knot in each eye, attaching the white felt to the purple as you do so.

7 Stitch the mouth with black floss and large straight stitches.

8 Use the white thread and the blanket stitch (or any stitch of your choice) to attach the edges of the eyes to the head.

9 Cut two little triangles from the white felt, and attach them just under the mouth with the white thread and small straight stitches.

10 Use the lime green thread and the blanket stitch to attach the lime green polka dots to the front of one body piece.

11 Place the embellished head on top of the second headpiece. Use the purple thread and the blanket stitch to attach the two pieces at the outer edges, starting at one bottom corner and stitching all the way around to the opposite bottom corner, leaving the bottom edge open.

12 Place the embellished body on top of the second body piece. Use the purple thread and the blanket stitch to attach the two pieces at the outer edges, starting at one bottom edge and stopping at the neck opening, then starting on the other side of the neck opening and stitching all the way around to the opposite bottom edge, leaving the top and bottom edges open.

13 Place the monster body over the soap dispenser. Place the head over the top of the dispenser by poking the nozzle through the nose slit. Press down on the head and....yuck!

Zombie Candy Corn Plushie

DESIGNER: JODIE RACKLEY

Straight out of
Children of the
Candy Corn, this
is one sweet treat
that bites back.

Basic sewing kit (page 9)

Templates (page 117)

4 colors of floss

3 shades of green felt: 1 sheet (9 x 12 inches [22.9 x 30.5 cm]) in a medium shade and scraps in two other shades, one lighter and one darker

Felt scraps in dark pink, light pink, black, white, and gray

1 button

Fiberfill

1 Pin the templates to the felt, and cut closely around the edge to make the shapes.
- Using template A, cut one shape from the medium green felt.
- Using template B, cut one shape from the lightest green felt.
- Using template C, cut one shape from the darkest green felt.
- Using template D, cut one shape from the medium green felt.
- Using the eye template, cut one shape from gray felt.

2 Match up the candy corn stripe felt pieces so that the top overlaps the middle and the middle overlaps on the bottom. The cutout for the mouth should match up perfectly if they are overlapped just right. Pin them together.

3 Cut the piece of black felt large enough so that it will cover the entire mouth opening. Cut a small half circle from the dark pink scrap, and stitch it in place toward the bottom of the black piece using matching floss. From the small scrap of white felt, cut a few small triangles for the teeth. If you need to, secure them with a few small stitches.

4 Sew a straight stitch across the edge of the top piece to attach it to the middle piece where the shapes overlap.

5 Line up the black mouthpiece behind the hole for the mouth. When you have it in the position that you like, pin it in place.

6 Stitch across the bottom of the middle piece, securing the middle to the bottom piece, stitching around the top edge of the mouth opening. Then using another piece of floss, continue to stitch around the bottom half of the mouth to secure the black mouth-piece in place.

7 Using the same technique, place the piece of light pink felt behind the shape you cut in the top of the corn. Place the pink felt behind the hole, pin it in place, and stitch around the outside edge of the shape until the pink piece is secured in place. Use a contrasting pink floss to make open loop stitches (or other stitches of your choosing) to resemble a brain.

8 Using the same color floss you used for the body, stitch the eye circle in place using a straight stitch. On top of the eye circle, add a button and use a matching thread to sew it in place.

9 With black floss, stitch a large cross stitch for the other eye and add a few stitched details.

10 Layer the finished candy corn front on top of the solid candy corn shape (template A), and pin it in place. Sew a straight stitch around the edge to start forming the plush, but when you get close to where you began, leave enough room to begin stuffing the plush.

11 Add fiberfill to the edges and corners first, and then work your way toward the middle and the open side. As you finish stuffing the candy corn, continue sewing the edge up until it is firmly stuffed and you've reached where you started.

Halloween Hair Clips

DESIGNER: JODIE RACKLEY

Having a bat hair day? This snaggle-toothed bat,
black cat, or sweet owl will dress up your do.

WHAT YOU NEED

Basic sewing kit (page 9)

Templates (page 122)

Blank barrette

TO MAKE THE BAT

Sheet of purple felt, 9 x 12 inches
(22.9 x 30.5 cm)

Purple, gray, or white (for the
mouth), and green (to match
the button eyes) floss

2 buttons

TO MAKE THE CAT

Felt scraps in black,
orange, and purple

Black, purple, orange, pink,
fuchsia, green (to match the
button eyes), and gray floss

2 buttons

WHAT YOU DO

To Make the Bat

1 Enlarge the templates and cut them out.
Cut one full-sized bat piece, two wings, one
teardrop shape for the body, and two small
triangles (for ears), all from purple felt.

2 Line up and pin the wing and body shapes
together; the body piece should overlap
the wings. With purple floss, sew a straight
stitch along both sides of the body just
where the sides of the wings are—we will
finish the rest later.

3 Using the purple floss again, sew a few
small straight stitches from the top point
on the wing to the first bottom point on the
wing and again from the top point to the
second point on the bottom of the wing,
making an upside-down "V" shape. Repeat
for the other side.

4 Sew the buttons on the bat's face with
green floss. Using the gray or white floss,
sew a few backstitches or one long straight

stitch to make the mouth. Stitch a "V" shape
with two small stitches to make a sweet
snaggletooth.

5 Working on the backside of full-sized bat
piece, sew the barrette in place. Stitch through
the circle hole on each end to hold the barrette in place, and then continue with several
stitches across the shaft of the barrette.

6 Layer and pin the front piece on top of the
back piece, matching up the edges. Place the
triangle bat ear shapes at the top of the head
in between the layers.

7 Starting at the bottom point of the body,
sew through both layers along the outside
edge of the whole bat shape using a straight
stitch, being sure to sew a stitch through the
triangle ears. Continue until you reach your
starting point.

Tip: Follow the same basic steps to create
the owl hair clip.

To Make the Black Cat

1 Use the templates to cut two cat-shaped pieces from black felt, one hat shape from purple felt, and one hatband from orange felt.

2 Place the orange stripe on the hat, line it up with the edges, and sew a few straight stitches across it.

3 Place the hat on top of one of the full-sized cat shapes. Using the purple floss, straight stitch on the bottom of the hat just to the start of curved edges.

4 Sew the clip in place on the backside of the other full-sized cat shape. Stitch through the circle hole on each end to hold the barrette in place, and then continue with several stitches across the shaft of the barrette.

5 To create the kitty face, sew the button eyes in place, and using one of the shades of pink floss, sew a "V" shape inside the ear. With the other shade of pink floss, sew the nose in between the button eyes, using satin

stitch to make a triangle shape and straight stitches to make an upside-down "V" shape for the kitty mouth.

6 To make the floss whiskers, knot one end of the gray floss and pull it through to the front. Knot the floss again on the front and cut off the remaining floss, leaving a small amount of the frayed thread behind. Separate the strands a bit to make the whiskers.

7 Layer and pin the front piece on top of the back piece, matching up the edges. Using purple floss, complete the stitching around the rest of the hat. Using black floss, stitch around the rest of the kitty shape, sewing closely along the edge and working from one side to the other.

Creepy Bug Cling-Ons

DESIGNER: KATHY SHELDON

This no-sew project just requires a bit of patient tracing and then snipping. Drape the pieces on a lampshade and watch what happens when you turn on the light.

WHAT YOU NEED

Basic sewing kit (page 9)

Templates (page 116)

Freezer paper (for transferring the templates)

2 black felt sheets, 9 x 12 inches (22.9 x 30.5 cm) (see Note)

Craft knife and craft mat

Note: You can use stick-on felt for this project if you want to permanently decorate a lamp shade, but regular craft felt will cling to most shades just fine.

WHAT YOU DO

1 Use the templates to trace the spiderwebs and bugs onto the smooth (non-waxy) side of freezer paper.

2 Cut around the shapes roughly, leaving a small border of the freezer paper.

3 Iron the freezer paper (waxy side down) onto the black felt. Cut out the shapes carefully and then remove the freezer paper. Use a craft knife and craft mat to cut out the smaller inside shapes on the spider web.

Tip: Extend the outer strands of the webs as long as you like.

4 Hang the spiderwebs and bugs on a lamp shade or another spot that needs a spooky accent.

Day of the Dead Mask

DESIGNER: SUZIE MILLIONS

Mexican tradition has it that the spirits of the dead visit their families for El Día de los Muertos on October 31 and leave on November 2. Hide the Halloween candy!

WHAT YOU NEED

Basic sewing kit (page 9)

Templates (page 114)

Black felt, about 7½ inches (19 cm) square

White, hot pink, yellow, bright green, and black self-adhesive felt

Elastic strap, two 8-inch (20.3 cm) lengths

Craft knife

Hole punches, ¹⁄₁₆ inch (1.6 mm) and ³⁄₁₆ inch (5 mm)

Note: Regular felt and craft glue can be substituted for self-adhesive felt.

WHAT YOU DO

1 Using the templates, cut out one skull back shape from black felt. Cut along the outer edges with scissors, and cut out the eyeholes with the craft knife. Punch the holes for the elastic strap as indicated on the template, using the smaller hole punch.

2 Cut out one skull front shape from white self-adhesive felt. Cut along the outside line with scissors, and cut out the eye socket holes and the nose with the craft knife.

3 Before removing the paper backing from the white skull, hold it in place over the black skull back to be sure the black piece is right side up (note: this pattern is not symmetrical). Insert the ends of the elastic straps through the holes you punched in the black skull. Remove the paper backing from the white skull and press it in place on the black one, positioning the ends of the elastic straps so they are sandwiched between the two layers.

4 Using the templates, cut out 11 large petals and 11 small petals from the pink self-adhesive felt. Lay them in place around the eyeholes, using the longer petals on the top and the shorter ones around the sides and bottom. Peel off the paper backing, and press them in place.

5 Cut out the other decorative pieces using the templates. Cut 10 teardrops, 2 leaves, and 2 strips cut from black self-adhesive felt; 2 fancy leaves from green self-adhesive felt;

and 2 hearts from yellow self-adhesive felt. Cut 13 dots from black self-adhesive felt using the larger hole punch.

6 Arrange all the pieces—except the "S" shapes (which you'll make with the thin strips of black)—on the white skull with the paper backing intact.

7 Once settled, start with the decorations on the cheeks, peeling off the backing and pressing them down.

8 Make the "S" scrolls. Remove the backing from the thin strips, and use the tip of the craft knife to scoot the piece into place, touching the strip as little as possible as you work to avoid tears.

Tip: Felt is like piecrust; the less you handle it, the better it comes out. If your "S" strip tears, press it down into position and slightly overlap the end of the piece you pressed down with the end of the piece that broke off, blend them together, and finish the "S".

9 Press down the rest of the decorations.

10 Clean up any fuzzy spots or loose fibers on your mask with the scissors. Viva los muertos!

Tip: Cutting a lot of self-adhesive felt pieces can leave your scissors fuzzy and sticky. As needed, scrub the blades with a steel wool soap pad, rinse, and dry thoroughly.

Felted Fall Acorns

DESIGNER: LISA JORDAN

WHAT YOU NEED

Acorn caps

Wool roving in Halloween colors

Soap (dish soap or olive oil soaps work nicely)

Water

Bowl or sink basin

Needle-felting mat and needle (optional, see step 3)

Fabric or white glue

WHAT YOU DO

1 Clean the acorn caps by swishing them briefly in a pan of water with a drop or two of dish soap in it. Rinse them and set them aside to dry on an old towel or newspaper (in the sun if possible) until they are completely dry.

Tip: Bake the caps in the oven for 20 minutes at 200°F (93°C) to be sure that no bugs have come along for the ride.

2 Pull off a tuft of wool roving, and roll it tightly into a ball. Pull another tuft of roving off and wrap it around the ball, trying to keep the shape somewhat round. Keep adding wool until the ball is about 50% larger than the desired size of the finished acorn body.

3 Submerge the ball in a bowl of hot water with a small amount of soap. Roll the ball gently between your hands, dipping it back into the hot water often. When the ball begins to hold together, it can be rolled

with more pressure. Add a drop of soap if it doesn't seem to be firming up. When the ball is the desired size and shape, rinse it by rolling it in cold water for a few seconds. Place the finished ball on an old towel to dry completely.

4 Glue the wool ball into an acorn cap, trimming the end if needed to help it seat firmly inside the cap.

Needle-felting is optional for these acorns. If you have the tools and wish to needle-felt, complete step 2 and then place the ball on the felting mat. Needle it on all sides with the felting needle, just enough to keep the layers in place. When needle-felting, focus on pushing the layers of wool to the center of the form, rather than all the way through it. This will make a firmer shape with a smoother surface.

The autumnal colors of these felted wool acorns will warm any room. Fall is the perfect time to gather the caps for this project.

Turn your felt scraps into child's play with these Halloween finger puppets.

Felt Finger Puppets

DESIGNER: KATHY SHELDON

WHAT YOU NEED

Basic sewing kit (page 9)

Templates (page 129)

Freezer paper (for transferring the templates)

FOR THE OWL

Felt scraps in tan, cream, and orange

Tan, brown, and orange embroidery floss

FOR THE SKELETON

White felt, 3 inches (7.6 cm) square

Black felt, two 4-inch-square (10.2 cm) pieces

White and black embroidery floss

FOR THE BAT

Brown felt scraps

Black and brown embroidery floss

FOR THE JACK O'LANTERN

Felt scraps in orange, brown, olive green, and black (the project shown uses black stick-on felt)

Olive green pipe cleaner

Olive green and orange embroidery floss

Black floss (if not using black stick-on felt)

FOR THE GHOST

Scrap of white felt

Black and white embroidery floss

WHAT YOU DO

To Make the Owl

1 Use the templates to trace all of the owl parts onto the smooth (non-waxy) side of freezer paper. Trace two each of the following: bodies, wings, eyes, and eyelids.

2 Cut around each shape roughly, leaving a small border of the freezer paper.

3 Iron the head, wings, and eyelids onto the tan felt. Iron the two bodies and the eyes onto the cream felt. Iron the beak onto the orange felt. Cut out each shape carefully, and remove the freezer paper.

4 Using the photo for reference, place the two eyepieces on the headpiece, and use the brown floss and a large French knot to attach each piece.

5 While you've got the brown floss out, make vertical straight stitches on the front of one body piece for embellishment. Set the body pieces aside while completing the next step.

6 Place the eyelids over the eyes, and use the tan floss and a straight stitch to attach the top curve of the eyelid to the head (leave the bottom of each eyelid unstitched).

7 Place the front (embellished) body piece on top of the back body piece, then arrange the two wings on the sides of the body front and the head at the top so it just overlaps the top of each wing.

8 Use the tan floss and the straight stitch to attach the wings and the head to the body (stitching through the body back). Start at one side of one wing and stitch to the same point on the other wing, making sure you leave a large enough opening at the bottom to insert a finger!

9 Place the beak on the body so the top is hidden under the head, and use the orange floss and tiny straight stitches to attach it.

To Make the Skeleton

1 Use the template and the freezer paper method to trace and cut out the skeleton from white felt. Transfer but ignore the red lines for now.

2 Before you remove the freezer paper from the skeleton, carefully snip on the red lines to give the skeleton details, using curved embroidery or manicure scissors.

3 Use small straight stitches and the white floss to attach the skeleton to the front of a piece of the black felt.

4 Use the black floss to make two large French knots for the skeleton's eyes and two small French knots for the nostril holes. Make the mouth with one large horizontal straight stitch and several small vertical stitches over it.

5 Place the other piece of black felt behind the front piece and cut (through both pieces of black felt) around the skeleton's shape, leaving enough of a black border to fit a finger.

6 Sew the two pieces of black felt together using the blanket stitch around the outer edge of the pieces, leaving the bottom open.

To Make the Bat

1 Use the templates and the freezer paper method to cut out two bodies, wings, and ears, all from brown felt.

2 Place the two body pieces on top of one another, with the edges of the wings and the bottoms of the ears sandwiched between the front and back body pieces.

3 Use black floss and small straight stitches to stitch the eyes and nostrils onto the head; then place the head onto the front body piece (it should just cover the top of the body).

4 Starting at one bottom edge of the body pieces, use the brown floss and the straight stitch to sew the front and back body pieces together, making sure you catch the edges of the wings and ears along with the top of the bat's head with your stitches. Leave the bottom open.

To Make the Jack O'Lantern

1 Use the templates and the freezer paper method to cut two pumpkin shapes from orange felt, the stem from brown felt, and four hands from green felt. From black self-adhesive felt, cut the eyes, nose, and mouth.

2 Use the orange floss and straight stitches to embroider the vertical ridges of the pumpkin body.

3 Remove the backing to attach the black stick-on felt pieces to the pumpkin.

Tip: If you're using regular black felt, attach the features with black floss and small straight stitches.

4 Cut the pipe cleaner into two 2-inch (5 cm) lengths.

5 Place two hand shapes together, and poke the end of one length of pipe cleaner between them. Use the olive green floss

and small straight stitches to sew the hands together, making your stitches look like leaf veins and attaching the pipe cleaner end as you stitch. Repeat with the remaining two hand shapes and pipe cleaner.

6 Place the two orange body pieces together. Poke the open end of each pipe cleaner into each side. Slip the bottom of the brown stem between the body pieces at the top.

7 Using the orange floss and the straight stitch, start at one lower edge of the pumpkin body and stitch around the outer edge to sew the front and back body pieces together, catching the pipe cleaner ends and the stem bottom in your stitches. Leave an opening at the bottom that's large enough to fit a finger.

8 Twist the pipe cleaner arms around a pencil one time.

To Make the Ghost

1 Use the template and the freezer paper method to cut out two ghost shapes from white felt.

2 Use the black floss to make two French knot eyes on the front of one ghost shape. Use the black floss and small straight stitches to make the mouth.

3 Place the ghost front on top of the ghost back. Use the white floss and the blanket stitch to attach the two pieces, leaving an opening at the bottom that's large enough to fit a finger.

Perfect for your little one-eyed Willy or Wilma, this patch has a tricky second flap that reveals a gruesome wound.

Pirate Eye Patch

DESIGNER: AMANDA CARESTIO

WHAT YOU NEED

TO MAKE ONE

Basic sewing kit (page 9)

Templates (page 120)

Felt scraps in black and skin tone

Scrap of bandanna fabric

Pinking shears

7 fake pearls, 5 mm

Red, gray, and black embroidery floss

White thread

Black elastic strapping, about 24 inches (61 cm)

WHAT YOU DO

1 Use the templates to cut out one patch shape from black felt and one slightly smaller patch shape (following the dotted lines on the template) from skin tone felt.

2 Pin the black eye patch to your bandanna scrap, stitch around the edge, and cut around the edges of the fabric with pinking shears.

3 In the center of the patch, stitch the seven pearls in place with white thread. Stitch two lines of straight stitch with red floss around the edge.

4 Transfer the template or use it as a guide to stitch the wound and the stitches in the center of the skin tone patch using gray and red embroidery floss.

5 Fold the top edge of the eye patch over by ½ inch (1.3 cm). Sandwich the top of the skin tone patch and the elastic strapping in the folded edge.

6 Stitch the casing in place with black floss and whipstitches.

Felt-o-ween

103

Make your Halloween party a graveyard smash with this not-so-spooky game. When you're not playing, the characters can double as puppets!

Monster Mash Ring Toss

DESIGNER: MOLLIE JOHANSON

WHAT YOU NEED

Basic sewing kit (page 9)

Templates (page 121)

Felt sheets (9 x 12 inches [22.9 x 30.5 cm]) in the following colors: 2 in black, 3 in white, 1 in brown, and 1 in purple

Green felt, 5½ x 4½ inches (14 x 11.4 cm)

Tan felt, 5½ x 4 inches (14 x 10.2 cm)

Light blue felt, 5½ x 3 inches (14 x 7.6 cm)

Red felt scrap

Black, white, green, tan, light blue, and red embroidery floss

8-inch embroidery hoop

¾-inch-wide (1.9 cm) fabric strips or ribbon, 2 yards (1.8 m)

Six 16 oz. water bottles

Fabric glue or hot glue

WHAT YOU DO

1 For each monster, cut two 9 x 5½-inch (22.9 x 14 cm) pieces of felt, and all of their extra pieces, using the templates and the photo as a color reference.

2 Appliqué the facial features and other extras in place on the monster fronts using three strands of matching floss and the blind stitch.

3 Pin the fronts and backs together, and stitch around the sides and top using six strands of contrasting floss and straight stitch. On Frankenstein's monster, place the neck bolts between the layers before stitching.

4 Wrap the fabric strips or ribbon around the inner piece of the embroidery hoop. Secure the ends with glue.

5 To play, slide a monster over each of the water bottles, and toss the embroidery hoop ring over them.

Batty Pillows

DESIGNER: DANA WILLARD

WHAT YOU NEED

FOR ONE 16-INCH-SQUARE
[40.6 CM] PILLOW
Basic sewing kit (page 9)

Template (page 122)

¾ yard (.7 m) of cotton fabric (or a ½ yard
[.5 m] of fabric for a small 12-inch-square
[30.5 cm] pillow)

¼ yard (.25 m) of felt in various colors

One 16-inch-square (40.6 cm) pillow form

Thread in various colors (to complement
the felt fabric colors)

Note: The amount of felt you'll need varies
depending on the amount of bats and color
combo you choose. ¼ yard (.25 m) is plenty
for three bats in one color.

WHAT YOU DO

To Make the Large Pillow

1 Cut one 16-inch-square (40.6 cm) front pillow piece and two 16 x 10-inch (40.6 x 25.4 cm) back pillow pieces.

2 Using the template, cut three bats from various felt colors. Fold your felt fabric, place the template on the fold, trace around the template with a marker or pen, then cut out the bat with sewing scissors.

Tip: When cutting out the bat shapes, make sure you cut away all the marker or pencil markings, so there aren't any black bits left behind.

3 Center three bats on the pillow front, and pin them in place. Or position two bats in a corner. Sew them to the pillow, using thread that coordinates with the felt color. Set the pillow front aside.

4 The two back pieces are going to overlap each other, creating an opening for the pillow form to be inserted. Start by finishing the overlapping edges of these back pieces. You only need to finish off one edge on each back piece. Iron one of the long 16-inch (40.6 cm) sides under ½ inch (1.3 cm), and then

iron under another ½ inch (1.3 cm) so the raw edge is tucked inside. Now sew down this edge, about a ¼ inch (6 mm) from the fabric edge. Do this on both back pieces.

5 To start putting the pillow together, first lay the front piece on your table with the right side facing up. Lay one of the back pieces on top of it, with the right side of the fabric facing down and with the finished edge in the middle of the pillow. Line up the other edges.

6 Now lay the other back piece on top of that, the same way as you did above, with the finished edge in the middle of the pillow. Pin the three layers together, all the way around the perimeter of the pillow.

7 Sew around the entire pillow using a ⅜-inch (1 cm) seam allowance.

8 Trim the corners of the pillow in the seam area, so they'll stick out better when the pillow is turned right side out. Then turn the pillow right side out. Push the corners of the pillow out using your finger, a chopstick, or something similar. Insert your pillow form.

These fun pillow covers feature envelope closures for easy seasonal swap outs.

Even candles can
dress up for Halloween.
Wrap your jar candle in
this cute cat costume, then light
the wick and watch the eyes glow!

Black Cat Candle Costume

DESIGNER: MOLLIE JOHANSON

WHAT YOU NEED

Basic sewing kit (page 9)

Templates (page 112)

Jar candle (see note on size below)

Black felt, about 6 x 13 inches
(15.2 x 33 cm)

Pink felt scrap

Tracing paper

Pink and white embroidery floss

¾-inch (1.9 cm) button

Note: Instructions are made to fit a
jar with a 4-inch (10.2 cm) diameter.
Adjust the length of felt you cut in
step 1 to fit your candle.

WHAT YOU DO

1 Using the templates, cut two ears and a tail from black felt and a nose from pink felt. Cut a 4 x 13-inch (10.2 x 33 cm) strip of black felt (or whatever size is needed to wrap around your jar candle).

2 Trace the face pattern onto tracing paper, then center it on the large black piece. Cut out the eyes from the felt. Using backstitch and all six strands of floss, embroider the mouth with pink floss and whiskers with white floss, stitching through the paper. Carefully tear away the paper. Stitch the nose in place using straight stitch.

3 Pin the ears in place along the top edge of the felt strip. Using three strands of white floss and straight stitch, stitch along the entire top edge, sewing the ears in place. Add a line of straight stitch along the bottom edge.

4 Wrap the costume around the jar candle, and pin the overlap. Remove the costume, and sew the ends together using straight stitch.

5 Sew the button on the back of the costume, near the bottom. Cut a slit in one end of the tail, and slide it over the button.

Templates

Bat Socks
Page 22 • copy at 100%

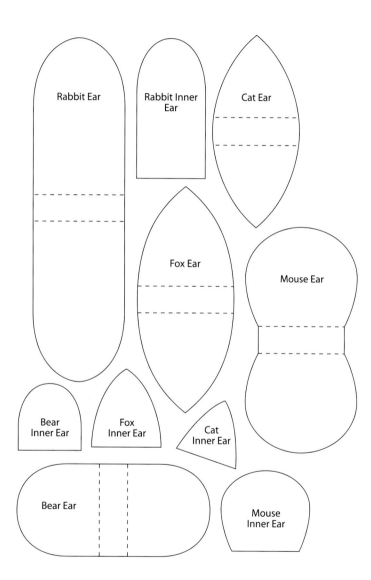

Rabbit Ear

Rabbit Inner Ear

Cat Ear

Fox Ear

Mouse Ear

Bear Inner Ear

Fox Inner Ear

Cat Inner Ear

Bear Ear

Mouse Inner Ear

Ears-to-You Headbands
Page 51 • copy at 200%

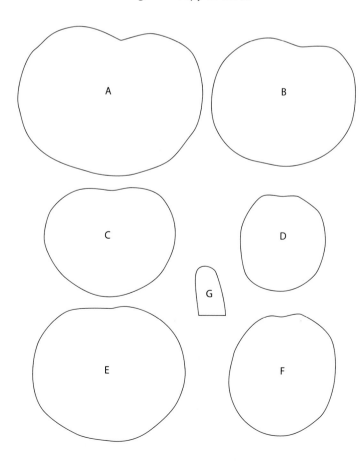

Pumpkin Napkins
Page 76 - copy at 125%

A

B

C

D

G

E

F

Felt-o-ween

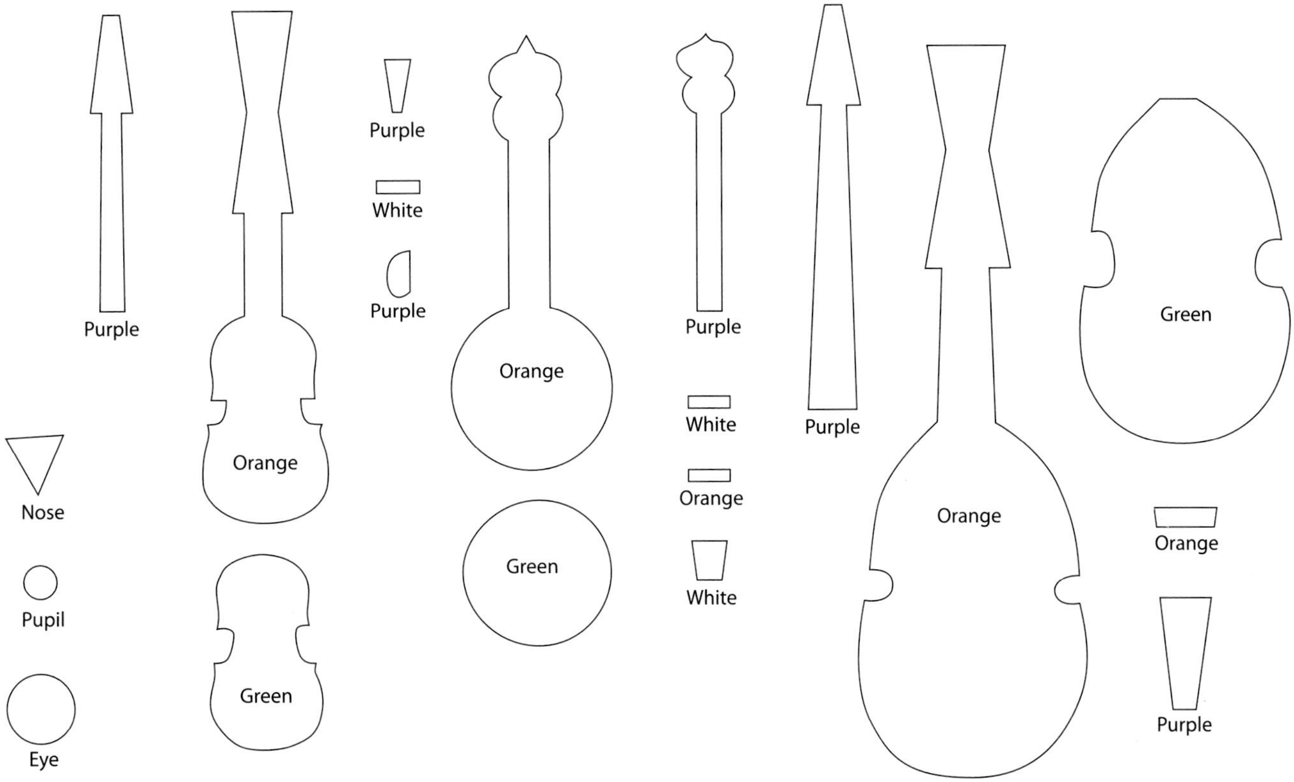

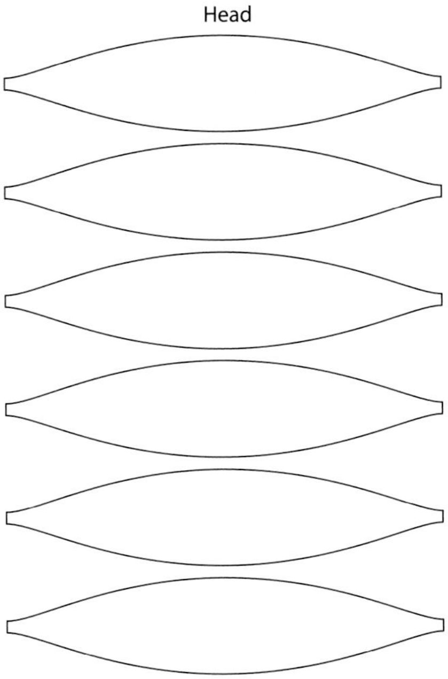

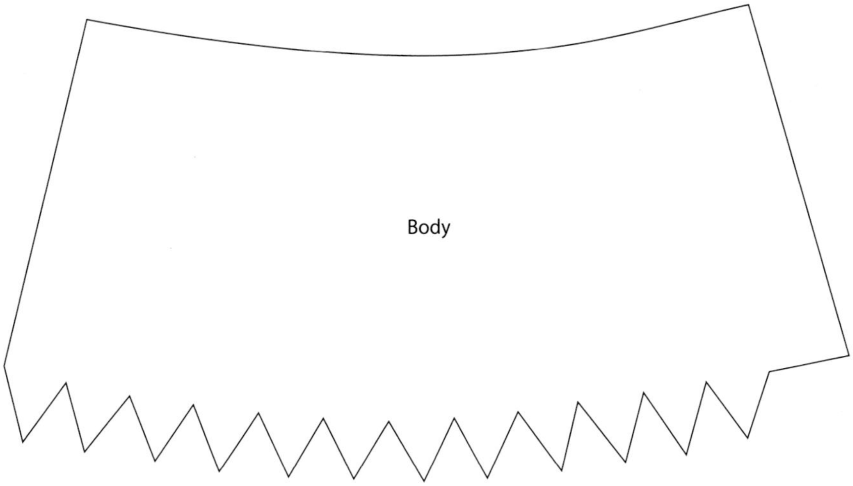

Purple

Purple

Purple

White

Purple

Nose

Orange

Pupil

Green

Eye

White

Orange

Orange

Green

Orange

Green

White

Orange

Orange

Purple

Head

Body

Purple

Purple

Pumpkin Patch Players
Page 67 • copy at 200%

Felt-o-ween

Leaf A

Leaf B

Leaf D

Leaf C

Spider legs

Spider

Spider eye

Bug A

Bug B

Bug C

Bug D

Bug E

Bug F

Creepy Crawly Wreath
Page 16 • copy at 200%

Top

(Outside edge)

Spiderweb

Black Cat Candle Costume
Page 108 • copy at 125%

Cat face

(cut slit)

Cat tail

Cat ear

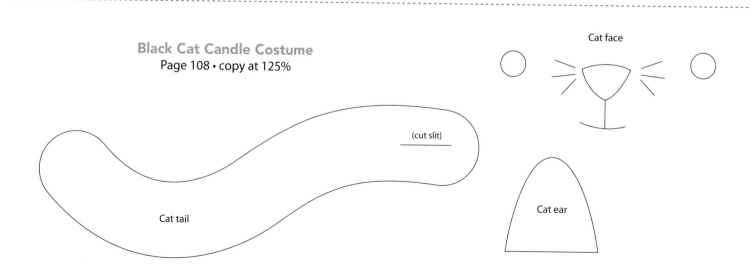

Undead Chokers & Bracelets
Page 80 - copy at 200%

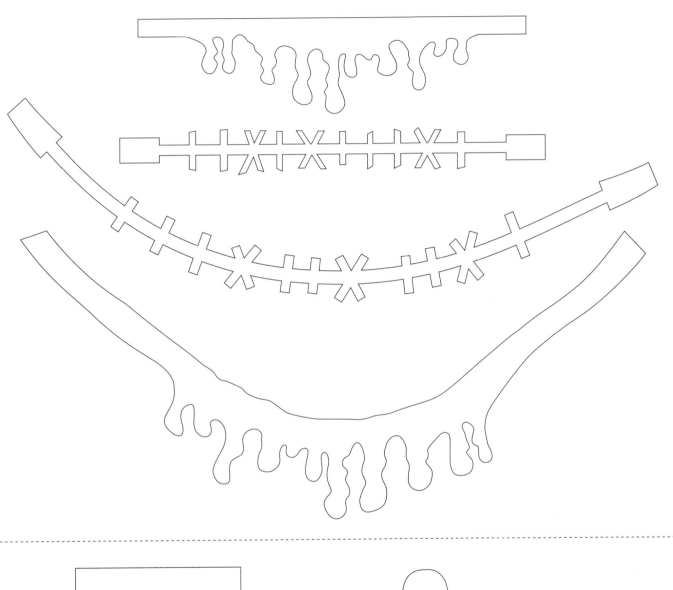

Bow A

Bow B

Bow C

Skull

Eye

Spooky Friends Wall Hanging
Page 34 • copy at 250%

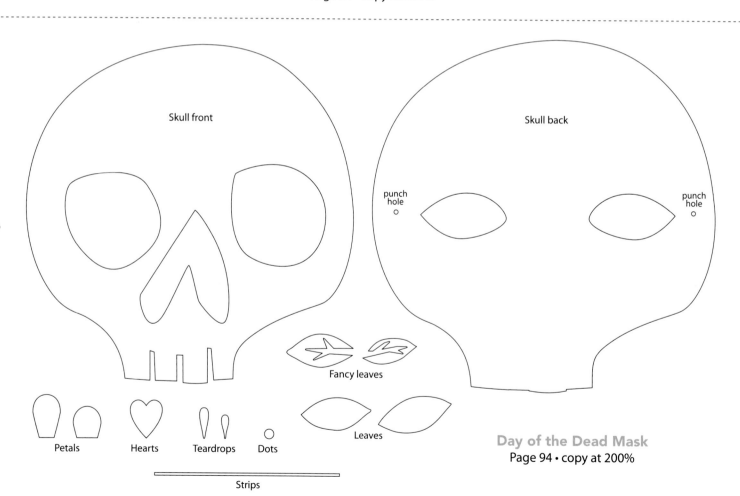

Skull front

Skull back

punch hole ○

punch hole ○

Fancy leaves

Petals

Hearts

Teardrops

Dots

Leaves

Strips

Day of the Dead Mask
Page 94 • copy at 200%

Gravestone

Hand

Ghost

Graveyard Cupcake Toppers
Page 43 • copy at 125%

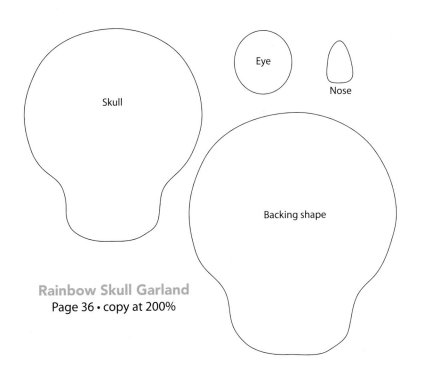

Skull

Eye

Nose

Backing shape

Rainbow Skull Garland
Page 36 • copy at 200%

Crow body

Crow beak

Scarecrow shirt

Scarecrow hat

Scarecrow head

Scarecrow pants

Silly Scarecrow Plant Picks
Page 58 • copy at 125%

Bat Mobile
Page 46 • copy at 200%

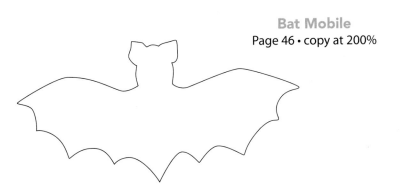

Felt-o-ween

Sew Gross Hand Warmers
Page 73 • copy at 200%

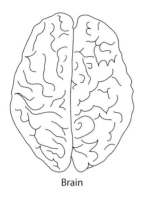

Brain

Finger

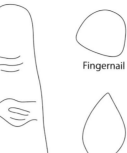

Fingernail

Opening

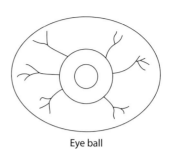

Eye ball

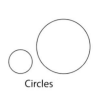

Circles

Creepy Bug Cling-Ons
Page 92 • copy at 200%

Punkin' Treat Pouch
Page 28 • copy at 200%

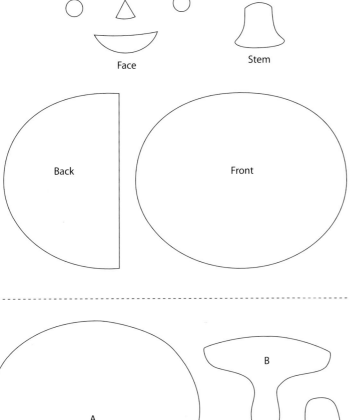

Face

Stem

Back

Front

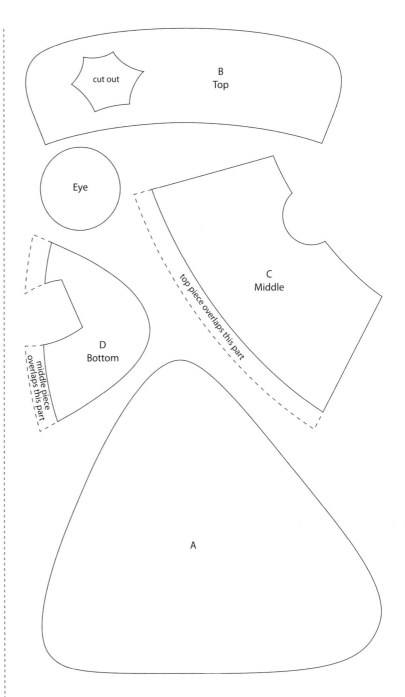

B
Top

cut out

Eye

C
Middle

top piece overlaps this part

D
Bottom

middle piece overlaps this part

A

Zombie Candy Corn Plushie
Page 87 • copy at 200%

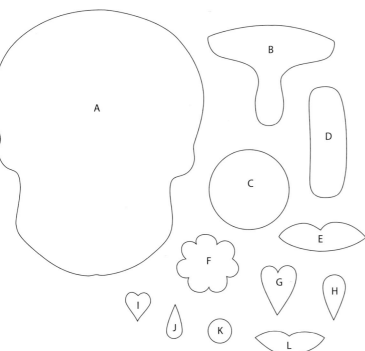

A

B

D

C

E

F

G

H

I

J

K

L

Day of the Dead Kid's Tee
Page 78 • copy at 200%

Felt-o-ween

Devil-Made-Me-Do-It
Pincushion
Page 41 • copy at 200%

Devil head

Devil body

Circle

Side

A B C

Flames

Candy Corn Bunting
Page 20 • copy at 125%

Flag

Bottom

Top

Middle

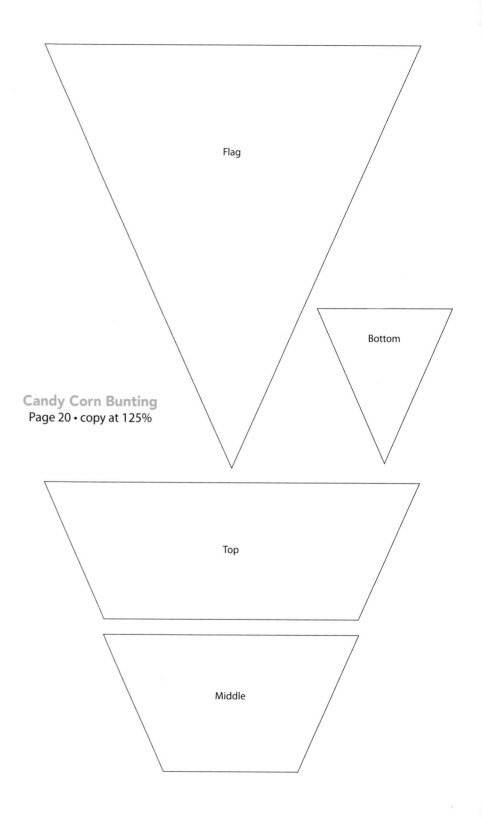

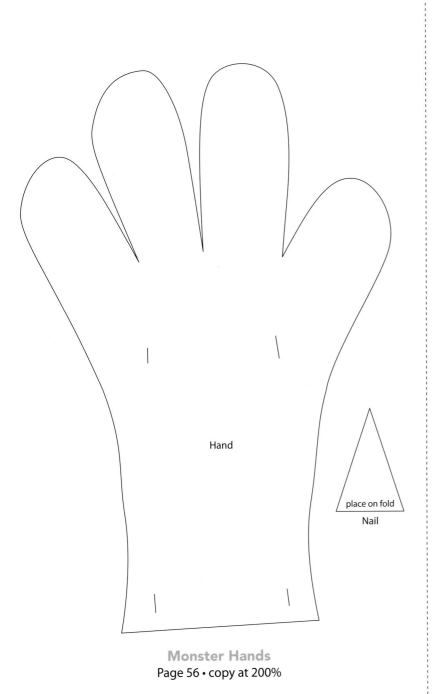

Hand

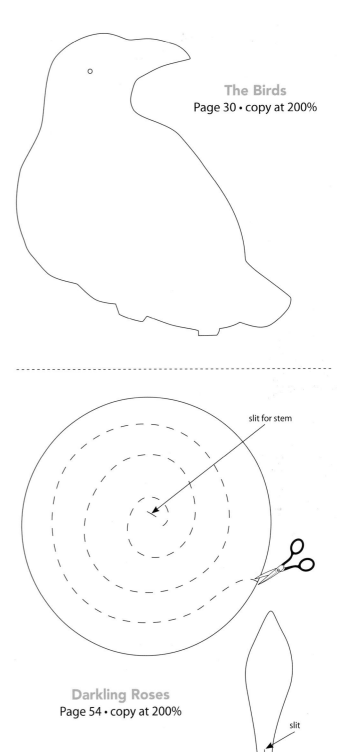

The Birds
Page 30 • copy at 200%

place on fold
Nail

Monster Hands
Page 56 • copy at 200%

slit for stem

Darkling Roses
Page 54 • copy at 200%

slit

place on fold

· Felt-o-ween

Pirate Eye Patch
Page 102 • copy at 125%

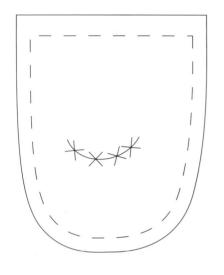

Wee Witch Booties
Page 32 • copy at 200%

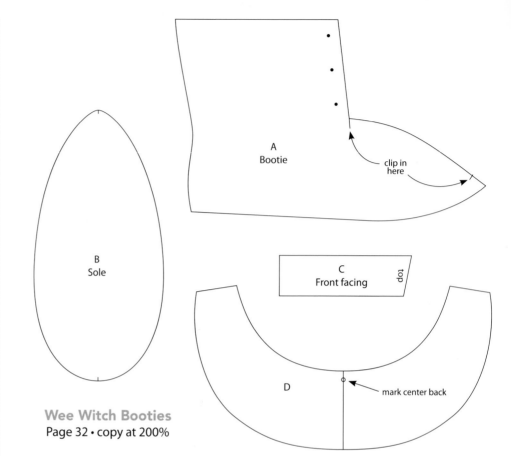

B
Sole

A
Bootie

clip in here

C
Front facing

top

D

mark center back

Oval

Oval

Eyes

Nose

Mouth

Cat

Pumpkin

Cat in Pumpkin Brooch
Page 62 • copy at 100%

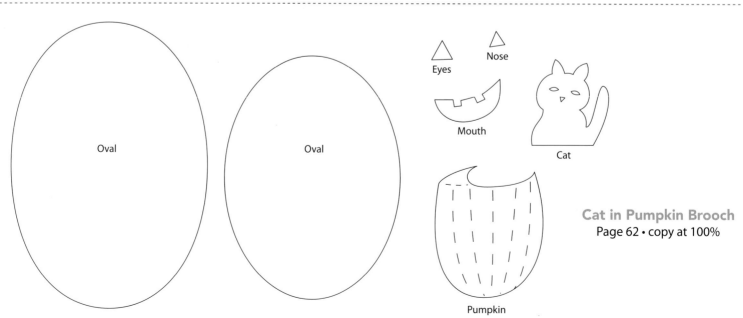

· Felt-o-ween

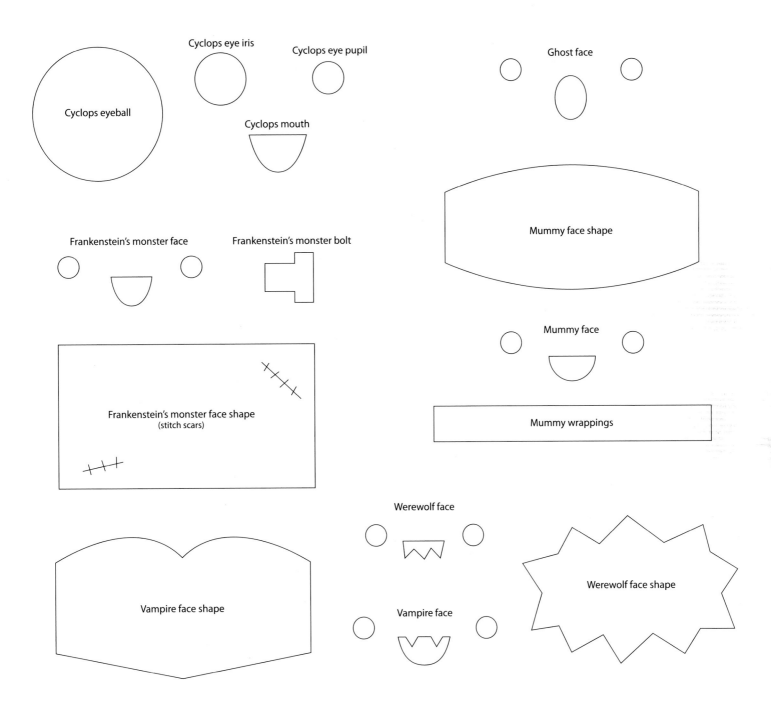

Cyclops eye iris

Cyclops eye pupil

Ghost face

Cyclops eyeball

Cyclops mouth

Mummy face shape

Frankenstein's monster face

Frankenstein's monster bolt

Mummy face

Frankenstein's monster face shape
(stitch scars)

Mummy wrappings

Werewolf face

Vampire face shape

Werewolf face shape

Vampire face

Halloween Hair Clips
Page 89 • copy at 200%

Owl

Cat

Cat hat

Hat band

Owl body

Owl wing

Bat wing

Owl head

Bat full

Bat body

Owl tail feathers

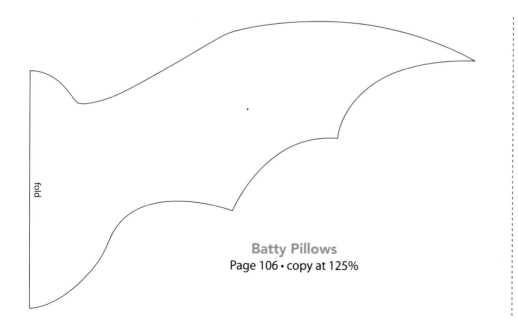

fold

Batty Pillows
Page 106 • copy at 125%

Ghosties Candle Mat
Page 26 • copy at 100%

Vampire Plushie
Page 38 • copy at 200%

Eye

Trousers

Vest
(back)

Hair
(front)

Hair
(back)

Vampire body

Cape

Vest
(front left)

Shirt

Vest
(front right)

Snotty Monster Soap Dispenser
Page 84 • copy at 200%

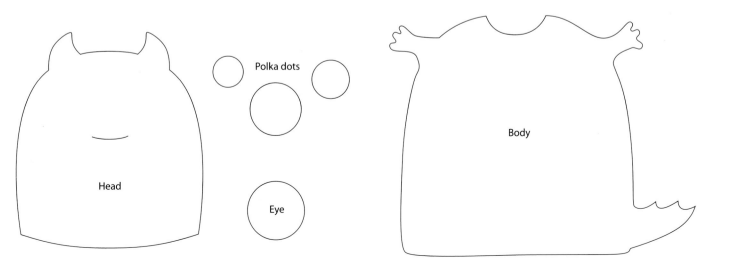

Polka dots

Head

Body

Eye

Monster Sugar Stash Bags
Page 60 • copy at 200%

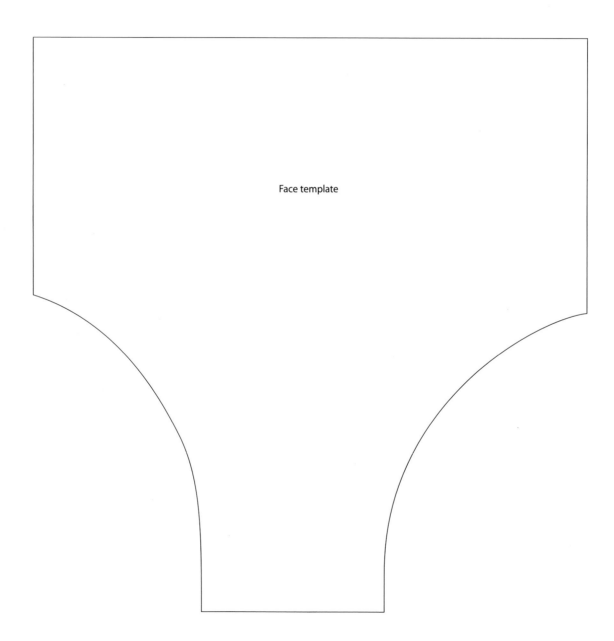

Face template

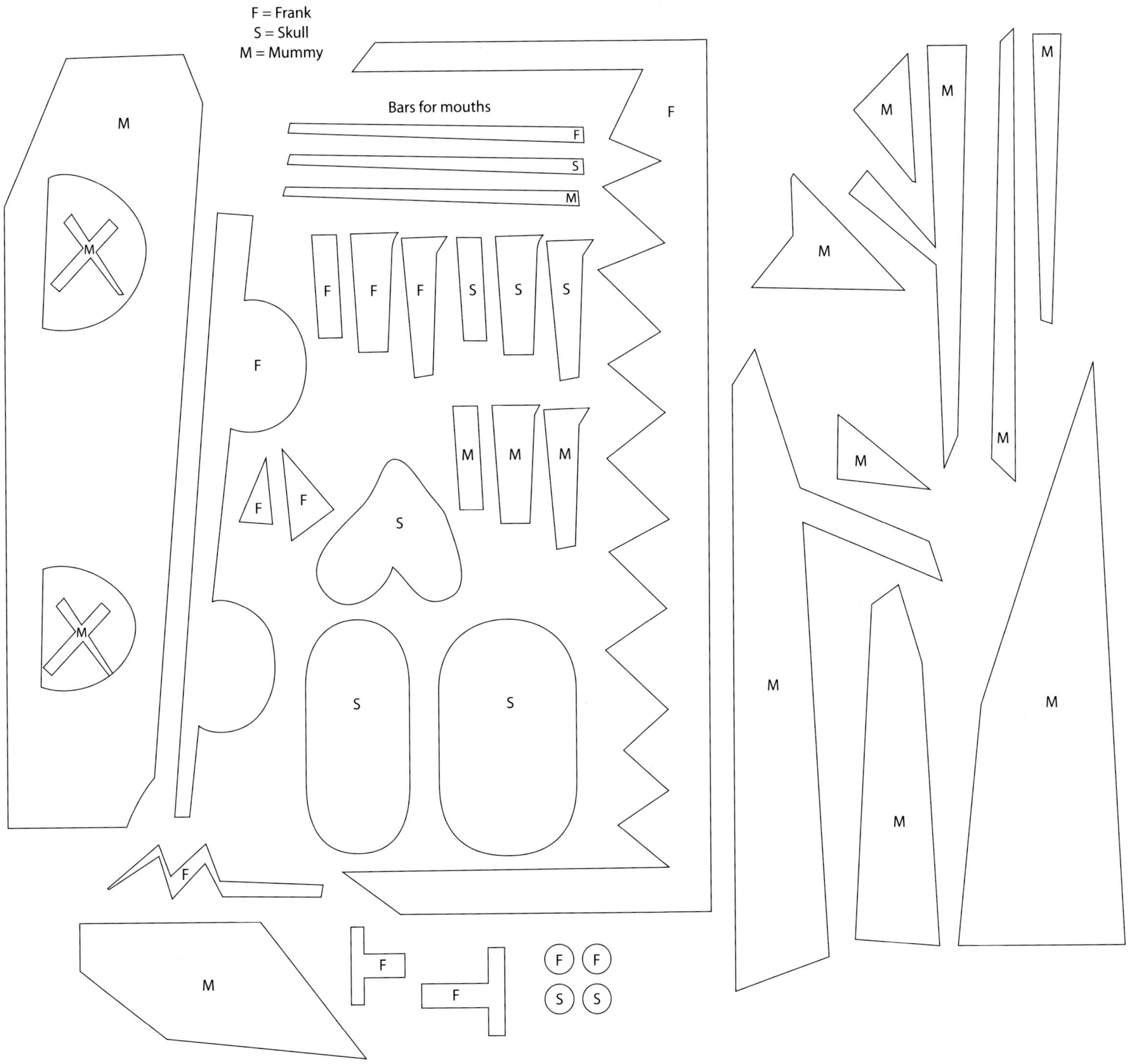

F = Frank
S = Skull
M = Mummy

M

Bars for mouths

F

F

F

F

F

F

S

S

S

M

M

M

M

M

F

F

F

S

M

M

M

S

M

S

S

F

M

F

F

F

F

S

S

M

M

M

M

M

M

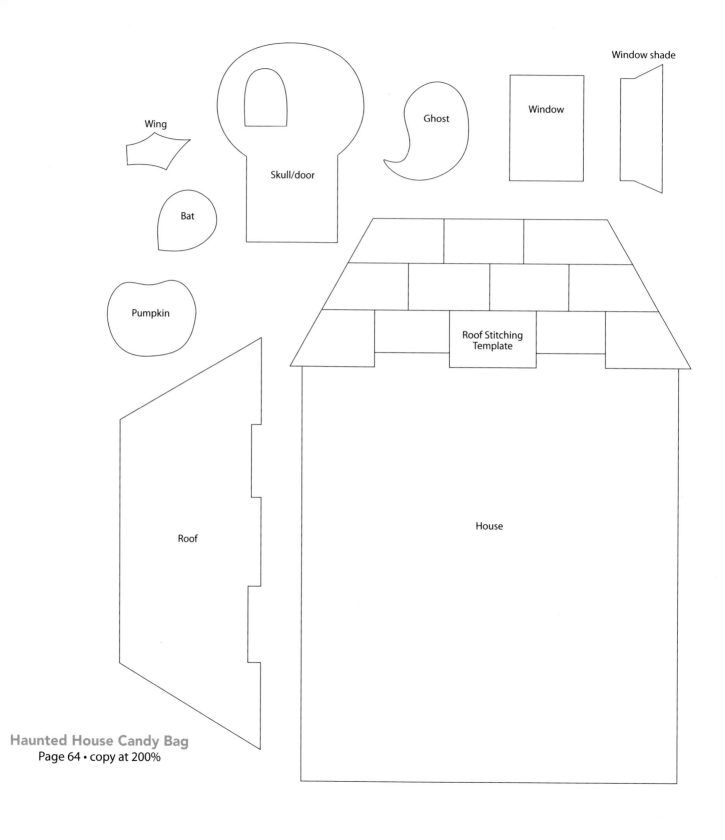

Wing

Skull/door

Bat

Ghost

Window

Pumpkin

Roof Stitching
Template

Roof

House

Haunted House Candy Bag
Page 64 • copy at 200%

Felt-o-ween

Wicked Sassy Fascinator
Page 24 • copy at 200%

No-Sew Halloween Bunting
Page 82 • copy at 125%

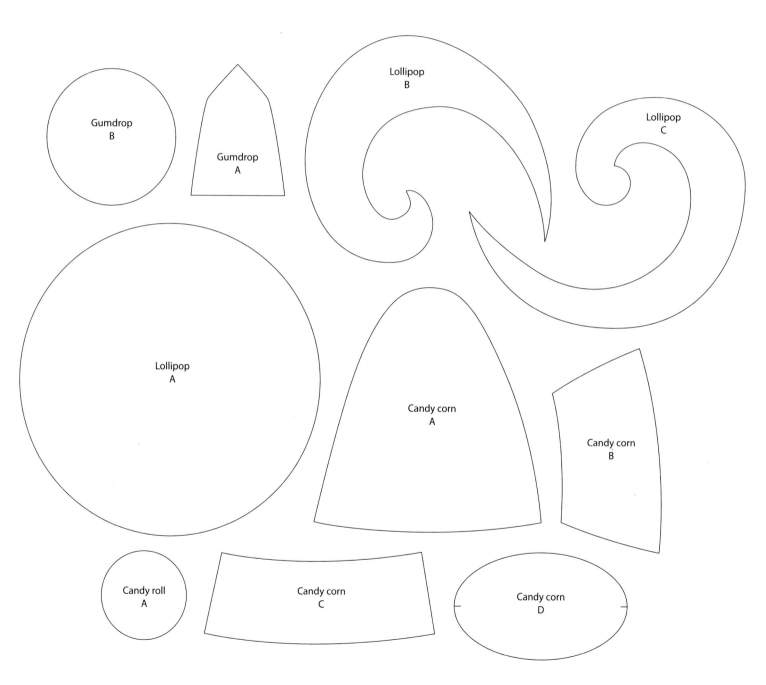

Felt Finger Puppets

Page 98 • copy at 100%

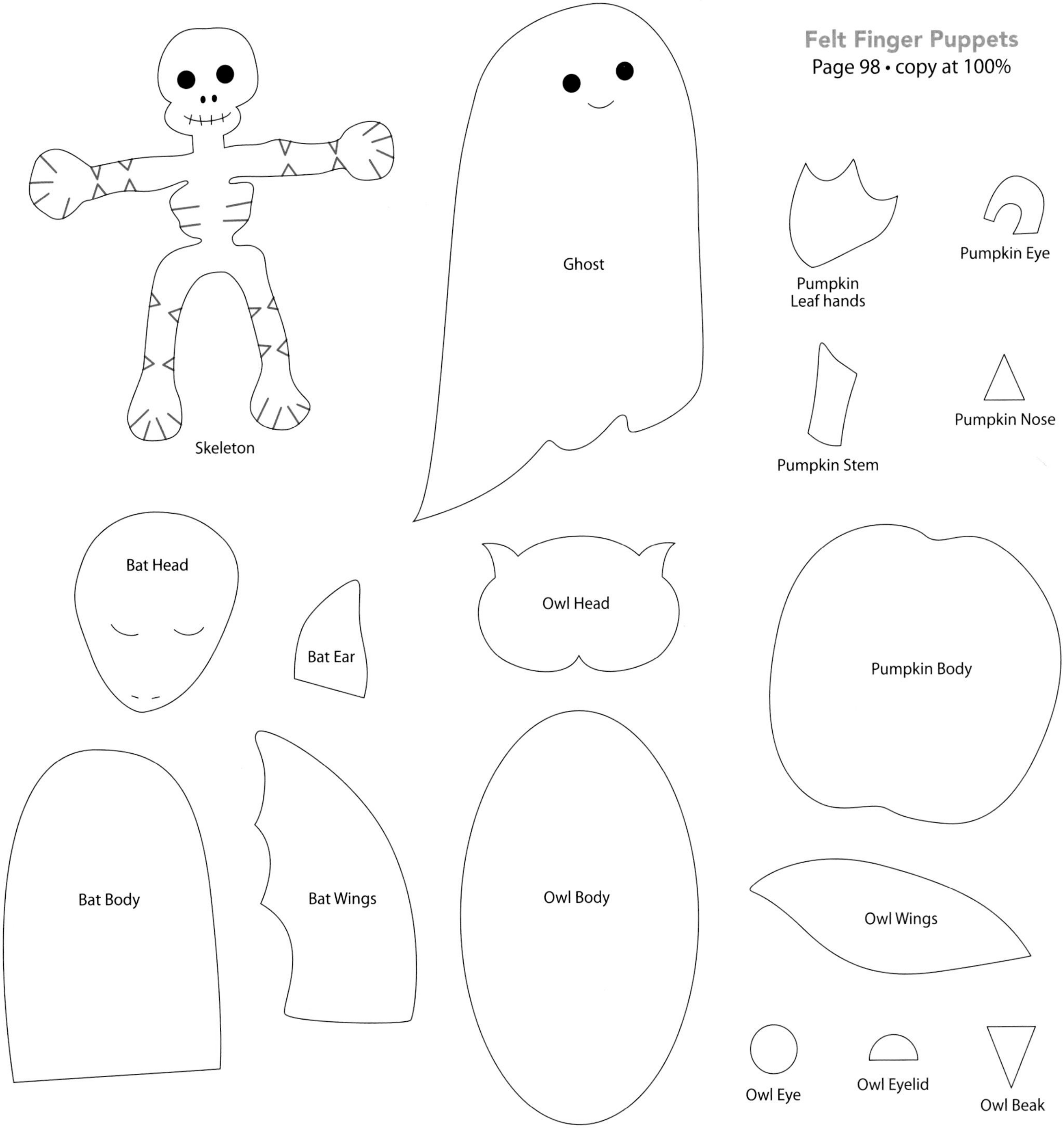
Skeleton
Ghost
Pumpkin
Leaf hands
Pumpkin Eye
Pumpkin Stem
Pumpkin Nose
Bat Head
Bat Ear
Owl Head
Pumpkin Body
Bat Body
Bat Wings
Owl Body
Owl Wings
Owl Eye
Owl Eyelid
Owl Beak

About the Designers

LAURA HOWARD

Laura is a designer, crafter, and author who likes to make and do…and is completely obsessed with felt! She's the author of two books about felt crafting: *Super-Cute Felt* and *Super-Cute Felt Animals*. Laura shares free tutorials and writes about her crafty adventures on her blog www.bugsandfishes.blogspot.com and sells her work at www.lupin.bigcartel.com.

MOLLIE JOHANSON

Mollie Johanson has loved cute things, creative messes, and cuddly critters for as long as she can remember. Her blog at www.wildolive.blogspot.com is known for embroidery patterns, simple stitched projects, and playful printables, most often featuring charming creations with smiling faces. Her work has been featured in *Mollie Makes*, *Australian Homespun*, and in a variety of books, including her own forthcoming title with Lark, due out in January 2015.

LISA JORDAN

Lisa Jordan is an artist living in rural Minnesota. Prone to tinkering with wood and wool, she's deeply inspired by nature and expresses her love of the odd and often overlooked bits of it through her work. She can be found blogging about her work and life out in the woods at www.lilfishstudios.com.

STEPHANIE LYNN LIEBERT

Stephanie Lynn Liebert has a passion for do-it-yourself decor, home projects, and anything that keeps her creative mind busy. She enjoys the challenge of designing projects on her own, preferably when using repurposed items. Her blog, www.bystephanielynn.com, is dedicated to inspiring others to find their inner creativity by sharing a variety of simple projects, fun crafts, and occasional recipes.

SUZIE MILLIONS

Suzie Millions is a cat-loving, vintage-dress-wearing artist and compulsive crafter who lives with her musician/letterpress printer husband, Lance, in a swinging 50s house in scenic Asheville, North Carolina. Her craft opus, *The Complete Book of Retro Crafts*, was published by Lark in 2008, and she's a frequent contributor to other Lark books (her Felty Family Portraits from *Heart-Felt Holidays* are featured on Martha Stewart's Living blog). Visit her at www.suziemillions.com and www.pinterest.com/retrosuzie/.

JODIE RACKLEY

Jodie Rackley is known for the bold use of color and simple designs that make up her handmade line, Lova Revolutionary (www.etsy.com/shop/lovahandmade). In 2012, she authored her first felt and embroidery craft book, *Happy Stitch: 30 Felt & Fabric Projects for Everyday*. She's currently working a line of embroidery and felt project patterns for her Etsy shop and loves creating in her home studio in a little town outside of Washington, DC.

CYNTHIA SHAFFER

Cynthia Shaffer (who shot the AWESOME photos for this book) is a photographer, quilter, and creative sewer whose love of fabric can be traced back to the age of six, when she learned to sew and in no time was designing and sewing clothing for herself and others. After earning a degree in textiles, Cynthia worked for 10 years as the owner of a company that specialized in the design and manufacture of sportswear. Numerous books and magazines have featured Cynthia's art and photography. She is the author of *Stash Happy: Patchwork* (Lark, 2011) and *Stash Happy: Appliqué* (Lark, 2012). For more information visit her online at www.cynthiashaffer.com or www.cynthiashaffer.typepad.com.

DANA WILLARD

Dana Willard authors the popular DIY sewing design blog, MADE (www.danamadeit.com), with eye-catching photography and easy-to-follow tutorials, giving a relatable voice to modern sewing. Her designs have been featured in various books, magazines, online communities, and in awards circles. Her first book, *Fabrics A to Z*, is essential for anyone who sews—beginner or experienced. Dana lives in the hot city of Austin, Texas, with her husband and three kids.

About the Authors

KATHY SHELDON

Kathy Sheldon writes, edits, and packages books. She grew up on a farm in New England, so making things by hand comes naturally to her. She's happiest when creating, whether it's a shrink plastic bracelet, a poem, a row of sweet peas, or a book about gardening or crafts. She is the author of many books, including *Shrink! Shrank! Shrunk!: Making Shrink Plastic Jewelry*, and the coauthor of *Fa la la la Felt!*, *Heart-Felt Holidays*, and *Aimee Ray's Sweet & Simple Jewelry*. When Kathy is not writing or creating in the mountains of Asheville, North Carolina, you can usually find her at her cottage in Maine, where she's the first to jump in the lake in the spring and the last one to leave the water in the fall.

AMANDA CARESTIO

Amanda's latest crafting obsessions include anything mid-century modern, making things for her new baby (she's on quilt number three currently!), and the fabulousness that is fusible web. When she's not bent over her sewing machine, editing a craft book, or exploring the Blue Ridge Mountains, Amanda enjoys spending quality time with her hubby, her sweet, sweet little girl, Miss Ruby, and her little brindle shadow, Violet. Amanda is the author of *Wee Felt Worlds* and *Never Been Stitched* (and other titles from Lark Crafts), and co-author of *Fa la la la Felt* and *Heart-Felt Holidays*. Her designs appear in several Lark Books; she blogs online at www.larkcrafts.com and at www.digsandbean.blogspot.com.

Index

Book Credits

Editors: Dawn Dillingham & Amanda Carestio
Art Director: Shannon Yokeley
Illustrators: Shannon Yokeley & Orrin Lundgren (templates)
Photographer: Cynthia Shaffer
Cover Designer: Shannon Yokeley

For more felt fun: